From
GOALS
To GROWTH

From GOALS *To* GROWTH

INTERVENTION & SUPPORT
IN EVERY CLASSROOM

LEE ANN JUNG

ASCD | Alexandria, Virginia USA

1703 N. Beauregard St. • Alexandria, VA 22311-1714 USA
Phone: 800-933-2723 or 703-578-9600 • Fax: 703-575-5400
Website: www.ascd.org • E-mail: member@ascd.org
Author guidelines: www.ascd.org/write

Deborah S. Delisle, *Executive Director;* Stefani Roth, *Publisher;* Genny Ostertag, *Director, Content Acquisitions;* Julie Houtz, *Director, Book Editing & Production;* Katie Martin, *Editor;* Sima Nasr, *Graphic Designer;* Mike Kalyan, *Director, Production Services;* Keith Demmons, *Production Designer;* Andrea Hoffman, *Senior Production Specialist*

Illustrations by Jason Bratcher. Photo credits: Monkey Business Images/Shutterstock ("Carmen" and "Danielle"), Jaren Jai Wicklund/Shutterstock ("Carter"), and Pressmaster/Shutterstock ("Maggie").

Note: An earlier version of this work was published by Solution Tree as *A Practical Guide to Planning Interventions & Monitoring Progress.* The author has expanded and updated the ASCD edition.

All web links in this book are correct as of the publication date below but may have become inactive or otherwise modified since that time. If you notice a deactivated or changed link, please e-mail books@ascd.org with the words "Link Update" in the subject line. In your message, please specify the web link, the book title, and the page number on which the link appears.

PAPERBACK ISBN: 978-1-4166-2598-8   ASCD product #118032   n3/18
PDF E-BOOK ISBN: 978-1-4166-2625-1; see Books in Print for other formats.
Quantity discounts are available: e-mail programteam@ascd.org or call 800-933-2723, ext. 5773, or 703-575-5773. For desk copies, go to www.ascd.org/deskcopy.

Library of Congress Cataloging-in Publication Data is available for this title.
LCCN: 2017057167

27 26 25 24 23 22 21 20 19 18   1 2 3 4 5 6 7 8 9 10 11 12

From GOALS To GROWTH

ACKNOWLEDGMENTS

Thank you to Robb Clouse for acquiring this book. His thoughtful work on behalf of all students, but especially those who receive intervention, is the reason this book is with ASCD. I'm grateful to have him as a colleague and, more important, as a friend.

REDEFINING STUDENT SUPPORT

For many years, the predominant way we provided intervention and instructional support followed a straightforward formula. We used ability grouping and, during core instruction, sent the students who needed extra support to a separate classroom. There, they worked with a specialist to pursue goals that were less rigorous or different from those in the general curriculum. And it all seemed logical. These students were working below grade level, so grade-level instruction felt inappropriate. The specialist or special education teachers were the intervention experts, so it seemed to make sense that students who needed intervention should be learning with them in a separate, dedicated classroom.

We now know that this model of "pull out and replace the curriculum" isn't effective for the students who need supplemental instruction and intervention. This model even impedes the growth of teachers and students who do not need extra support.

The effective model for delivering supports contrasts from this segregated approach. It is *inclusive,* and this means so much more than the location for support. Truly inclusive supports require classroom teachers and specialists to work as a team to embed evidence-based practices in the general education classroom. This elevates the quality of instruction that *all* students receive. When students with a broad range of abilities and learning profiles are all taught together, the general education teacher gains new strategies, the specialists gain a deeper understanding of the curriculum, and the students receive more comprehensive support—meaning fewer of them need supplemental instruction or intervention. This approach also promotes a school culture in which students who struggle don't "belong" to special education or specialists; instead, *all students belong to all teachers*. Win, win, and win!

There's just one catch: implementing a team-based approach to designing instruction and intervention is complex, and it's not something that most teacher education programs have prepared educators to do.

This book presents a process that the members of interdisciplinary teams can use to select meaningful goals with students that truly provide access to the general curriculum and are gateways for a successful life. You will learn how to create support strategies to be used in every classroom and how to set up and use a scale that simplifies progress monitoring and allows all team members to easily measure student progress toward goals within the context of everyday classroom routines and activities. You will learn how to use your time as a team to make decisions based on the data you collect. You will gain the tools you need to create research-based growth plans for students—plans that will foster their success and make your job easier. Whether you are a general education teacher, special education teacher, educational leader, or related service provider, this book will provide you with practical tools to use in effectively supporting every student who has individualized or personalized goals.

Overview of the Growth Plan and the Planning Process

In her video, *Disability Is Natural*, Kathie Snow (2014) defines disability labels as "sociopolitical passports to services." It's an apt description. In the United States, a student must meet disability criteria outlined in state and federal law to qualify for special education services. Too often, students without identified disabilities cannot access the intervention and support they need.

The approach to growth planning in this book reflects my belief that all students who struggle with critical skills, regardless of diagnosed learning difference, deserve to have research-based, systematic support plans and a team that is committed to their success. Although the process of developing growth plans integrates seamlessly with a school's existing individualized education program (IEP) and response to instruction and intervention (RTI^2) structures, it can—and should—be used for every student who needs support or intervention on a critical skill, not only those who qualify for special education services. Furthermore, this process supports a personalized learning approach that can benefit *every* student.

The Plan's Components and Format

The kind of growth plan we'll discuss in this book offers more detail than what is found in an IEP and more rigor of measure than is often found in personalized learning plans. It is designed to be used by teams of educators, families, and specialists working together. The plan includes five components: (1) the annual goal, (2) the settings in which intervention is delivered and progress is measured, (3) a scale for measuring performance, (4) the intervention and support strategies the team will use, and (5) a visual representation of data showing growth over time.

This book explores the components of the growth plan in detail and provides practical examples of how these plans are assembled. It's a process that involves asking and answering a lot of questions.

This questioning is essential. A study I conducted in 2010 showed that embedding targeted prompts within a growth planning form can yield significant improvements in the quality of the plans teams develop (Jung, 2010). These results were evidence that the form really does matter, and they started me on a six-year iterative process of developing and refining a growth planning form and online platform. Each design decision about the growth plan, from where fields appear, to the colors of the data map, to the layout of the scale for measurement, was a purposeful response to iterations of feedback from educators who were using it. Figure 1.1 shows an example of my growth plan format.

The completed growth plans in this book are illustrated with screenshots from the online platform GoalWorks® (GoalWorks.org). As a web-based platform, it includes features to support easy team communication and collaboration in real time. Although this online collaborative tool and others like it certainly add value, it's important to stress that *the growth planning process in this book does not require any special technology*. It reflects best practice for designing intervention and support and measuring progress.

The Planning Steps

No matter the tool or form that teams use, the practice of growth planning includes the following steps (see Figure 1.2):

1. Select critical skills to target.
2. Determine the settings for intervention and measurement.
3. Outline the increments of growth in a goal attainment scale.
4. Write the annual goal.
5. Develop interdisciplinary strategies.
6. Use data from implementation to inform instructional decisions.

FIGURE 1.1 GROWTH PLAN EXAMPLE

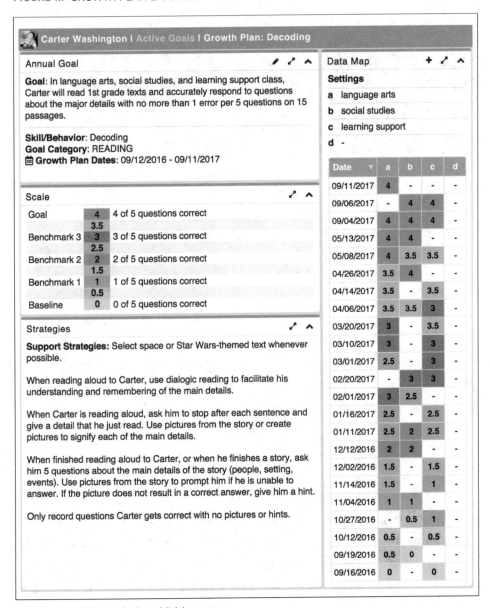

For a reproducible growth plan, visit lajung.com.

FIGURE 1.2 GROWTH PLANNING PROCESS

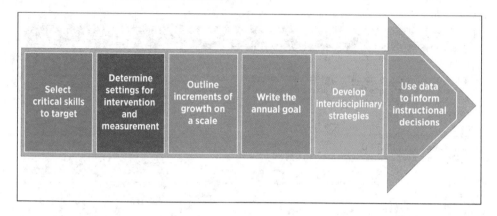

These six steps lead teams to develop meaningful plans for student growth on critical skills. We'll delve into the details of each step in the chapters ahead.

Team Members and Their Roles

The growth planning process is an interdisciplinary one—one that brings everyone's great ideas to the table to co-create a meaningful and effective plan for growth. This process assumes all members of the team have a valuable perspective and a voice that is necessary to the process. Let's explore the team members and their roles in the process of growth planning.

General Educators

As we shift student support from a specialist-driven model to a team-driven one, the role of general educators becomes especially important. General educators know the curriculum the best and can speak to the expectations for the grade level. Classroom teachers spend more time with students than any specialist, particularly at the elementary level, and they are likely to bring greater knowledge of a student's strengths, interests, and nuances. Critically, these educators are well positioned to describe the student's performance *in context*. For students with IEPs, they can furnish richer and more meaningful information than any standardized instrument can provide. For example, a student struggling with language would be better served by a vocabulary list generated by her areas of interest and from her own writing or from her content-area teachers than by a generic one. The tailored list would focus the student on mastering the words that she needs to keep up with immediate learning, stay on track in various parts of the curriculum, and follow personal interests.

As a reminder, the Individuals with Disabilities Education Improvement Act (IDEIA, 2004) requires that every IEP meeting includes certain people: someone who represents the local education agency, a person who can interpret the eligibility evaluation, a special education teacher, family members, the student, anyone the family chooses to invite, and *a general education teacher*. Although just having a general education teacher in the room during the IEP meeting is enough to satisfy the letter of the law, IDEIA includes the requirement to ensure that eligible students will have *access to the general curriculum*. Input from general educators—those best equipped to guide the team's conversation about the general curriculum—is essential to satisfy this requirement. Although there is no legally mandated growth planning process for students who don't qualify for special education, the same principle applies, and the same approach makes sense for every student.

Specialists

Traditionally, the role of the specialists has been to drive the IEP meeting for students who have IEPs. Specialists have typically been expected to arrive at the IEP meeting having selected the skills to target and with draft goals in place. Understandably, the resulting IEPs have tended to emphasize "special education goals" and "speech goals" rather than *the student's goals*. What these specialist-driven goals are often missing is the full context that will make them relevant to the student's priorities and the targets of the general education curriculum.

The interdisciplinary approach to growth planning may change the specialists' roles a bit, but it does not diminish it or discount their expertise. It relies on specialists' knowledge to help diagnose the origin of students' struggles and design the proper, research-informed support that all members of the team will provide.

Parents and Caregivers

The *I* in IEP stands for *individualized*, and giving students and parents a seat at the design table is an essential component to ensure that the IEP and growth plans are individualized. What are the student's unique interests, personality characteristics, dislikes, motivators, and preferences? What skills will help the student achieve what matters to him or her? Parents and caregivers play an essential role in planning student support and intervention, whether or not the conversation takes place as part of a formal IEP meeting. Although educators may be expert in their individual discipline and have valuable information to contribute on learning differences and how learning differences manifest in the classroom, parents and family members are the top experts when it comes to their child. They complete the picture, and the information they have should be integrated with every piece of planning (Bailey, Raspa, & Fox, 2012). Including caregivers is a way to ensure the discussion will never be just a listing of scores and services, but a compassionate conversation about a specific student and the best ways to support that student's success.

Although the family is a critical part of the planning team, they do not always know how to participate or even what their overall role in support is. Some parents find IEP or intervention meetings intimidating—as though they are on someone else's turf and expected to speak someone else's language. Consider, too, that some parents may have negative feelings and experiences associated with school and feel uncomfortable—unqualified even—to participate in discussions of school achievement. To school personnel, these parents' reticence during IEP or intervention meetings can read as disengagement. But which is more likely to be true: that these parents do not care about their children; or that they feel intimidated, believe they have little to contribute, or do not expect their input will be valued?

We must make it clear to parents or other custodial guardians that they are incredibly important members of the team and that we recognize them as the ultimate source of expertise on their children. And we must honor this arrangement by offering clear invitations and support for their participation, listening to their input, and putting it to use.

Students

Students should be involved in and driving the full growth planning process to the greatest extent that they are able.

Oftentimes, teams choose not to involve younger students because this would mean telling these students that they have a learning difference or that they need support to be on grade level. Although the intent is generally coming from a place of protecting the student, this decision is more often influenced by what will make the adults comfortable. It can be difficult to talk in child-friendly and positive terms about these topics.

The truth is, we are not tricking students by avoiding direct discussion of their struggles or differences. Most students know when they are behind grade level, and excluding them from discussions of what they need to work on can bring shame to their performance. Students should never feel shame about their performance! And all students should be fully aware of their strengths, the areas they need to target, and the steps being taken to support them.

Consider, too, that students have insight and opinions that can be valuable to teams working to select target skills for growth. They often know what supports or circumstances work well for them, what does not work, and what they would like to accomplish. We just have to ask them! By listening to students with sincerity, we show them the respect they deserve and identify them as the most important member of the team. They are the ultimate consumers of the services we provide.

Frequently Asked Questions

As teams prepare to implement this growth planning process with students, they may have questions about how it will operate within existing intervention processes. I'd like to take some time to discuss the questions I hear the most.

If a student qualifies for special education services, do we need to devise a growth plan in addition to the IEP?

There are distinct advantages to doing so.

Any student can achieve below grade level and need additional support, but the students many of us think of first when we hear "intervention" are those who qualify for special education services through the Individuals with Disabilities Education Improvement Act (2004). Roughly 13 percent of students in the United States receives one or more special education services (National Center for Education Statistics [NCES], 2013). The embrace of inclusion means these students are spending a decreasing proportion of their school time in segregated classrooms (Data Accountability Center, 2010). Because nearly every general education classroom today includes students who qualify for special education, it makes sense for the responsibility of planning instruction and intervention for students with learning or behavior differences to reside with an interdisciplinary team of specialists and general educators working together.

All students who receive special education services under IDEIA must have an individualized education program, or IEP. The IEP documents the student's eligibility for special education; his or her annual goals; the accommodations, modifications, and special strategies the student requires; and the support services the student will receive. Although the IEP includes a list of these supports, it seldom includes sufficient detail for everyone on the team to be able to implement the associated strategies on a day-to-day basis. Yes, the IEP team does need to outline the specific strategies to promote consistency of the program's implementation, but the IEP is probably not the best place for this level of detail.

IEPs are contracts that provide the broad framework for intervention. Because each is a legal document, changing it in any significant way requires a meeting and signatures from all team members. Contrast this formal process with the practical reality of the classroom, where teachers and specialists need the flexibility to choose a set of strategies, try them, and then make additional changes based on emerging student data. A supplemental growth plan that lives outside the IEP is a sensible way for team members to gain specificity on its implementation while retaining the fluidity necessary to ensure the support remains effective. In other words, the growth plan complements the IEP but serves a different purpose. Similarly, the IEP provides the broad legal framework for intervention that complements the development of a detailed and practical growth plan. In fact, the IEP process of writing goals should *begin* with the growth plan structure, not the other way around. One of the reasons teams struggle to implement IEP strategies and measure students' progress is that the IEP goals are often written in isolation by specialists and then brought to the IEP meeting for approval. This leads to a very different goal from one that is developed by an interdisciplinary team following the six steps I've described.

For clarification, consider the two goals in Figure 1.3. Which one makes the most sense to you? Which one seems like a goal that can be measured easily in everyday classroom settings and as part of everyday classroom assignments? And which one seems like a goal that you might typically find on an IEP?

Goal A is a pretty typical IEP goal. It includes a percentage, which makes the goal seem measurable. (That percentage is 80 percent, which many think of as "mastery." We will get to the concept of percentages later in the book.) But is it clear *what* exactly is being measured in this goal, and *how* it would be measured?

FIGURE 1.3 TRADITIONAL GOALS COMPARED WITH INTERDISCIPLINARY GOALS

Goal A	Goal B
Written by a specialist based on assessment data.	*Written by the interdisciplinary team based on assessment data and current expectations in general curriculum settings.*
Martin will plan organized and clear writing with depth and citations when appropriate on 80% of opportunities with fewer than three prompts.	On writing assignments of five paragraphs or more in language arts, government, and sociology, Martin will include an introduction, at least three supporting details in each paragraph, a variety of descriptive words and phrases that add depth, and appropriate citations on 10 assignments in a row.

Would all of Martin's teachers—specialists and classroom teachers—measure his progress toward Goal A in the same way? Is it even clear that this goal should be measured in general classroom settings? Would general education teachers even know how to measure it?

In contrast, Goal B provides enough clarity and specificity to support both effective planning and, critically, effective progress measurement and monitoring across disciplines and educators. Historically, states' area of lowest compliance with IDEIA is progress monitoring (Etscheidt, 2006). Getting our goals and measurements right is essential, and Goal B's interdisciplinary approach supports these efforts.

Should we go through this process for students who need extra support but don't have IEPs?

As noted, students who have diagnosed learning differences are not the only students who may struggle with certain skills and benefit from support and close monitoring. Most classroom populations include great variation in knowledge and proficiencies. Some students may be above grade level on a particular skill, and others significantly behind. Not just many but *most* of the students who are struggling with a critical skill do not qualify for special education services and have IEPs. Some of them may narrowly miss the criteria for eligibility; others may be experiencing temporary lags in performance. Still others may struggle as a result of interrupted formal education or inadequate instruction in previous years.

Even though some of these students may be many grade levels behind on one or more skills, their learning differences have an environmental basis, not a neurological one. Under IDEIA, adequate instruction is a necessary exclusionary criterion for classification as having a learning disability (the most common disability category) (Fletcher, 2006). In other words, the cause of the student's underachievement must be neurological in nature and not a result of the student's being an "instructional casualty."

Every student who is underachieving requires systematic instruction and support, regardless of the origin of the learning difference. Each of these students can benefit from a growth plan designed by a team of educators, regardless of whether he or she qualifies for special education services. Furthermore, the process of growth planning is one that is beneficial to *any* student who has individualized or personalized goals. And doesn't every student deserve personalized goals?

Our school is already using a specific intervention program for certain skills. Is using growth plans an *additional* intervention program?

The growth plans described in this book are not an intervention, per se. Nor does the growth planning process require the use of a particular curriculum or program. Instead, the growth plan is a *framework* that guides the development and individualization of intervention and support strategies, collection of data, and communication of progress made in response to instruction and intervention. For students with IEPs, this process bridges the gap between the IEP meeting and what happens day to day in the classroom. For students who do not have

IEPs, the growth planning process offers a systematic approach to instruction and support and is compatible with any evidence-based program or curricula.

How many goals and growth plans should a student have?

When teams convene to plan support for a student who is behind grade level, it can be tempting to set goals for every skill for which the student is behind. The growth planning process, however, is a deep dive into each goal. It would be difficult to design more than a few growth plans with each student. In this process, we prioritize our efforts, choose the most meaningful skills, and do an excellent job of designing and implementing support rather than try to cover every skill where the student might benefit from support and be unable to address them adequately or consistently.

So what is the right number of goals and growth plans? The answer depends on the student and on the context. For some, the answer is only one plan. Most will need two or three. Some may need five, but if you go much beyond this number, things will become difficult to manage. In the case of growth plans, more is not better; *better* is better.

Will using this growth planning process help us minimize the challenges we currently experience when writing IEPs?

The process described in this book is designed to help teams arrive at meaningful goals, plans for growth, and ways to measure progress. As such, it's set up to minimize the many challenges that busy teams face when they commit to helping all students achieve and differentiating instruction within their broader planning and teaching responsibilities. Having said that, this is complex work, and it's inevitable that challenges will arise. For each step in the growth planning process, I highlight a common challenge teams face and provide tips to prevent or respond to it.

Although it would be easy to write scenarios with fairytale endings, we all know that the real world is messy. There is a theme, though, to the prevention and successful response to each of the challenges I highlight: *an interdisciplinary focus.*

It is natural for general education teachers to think that the special education teachers have most of the intervention answers. And it is logical for the special education teachers to assume that the general education teachers know the curriculum and students the best, and, thus, that *they* should have most of the answers. We would all do well to remember that the parents have *many* answers, as do the students themselves. The best course of action is for us all to work as a team and incorporate each person's unique and valuable knowledge into the problem-solving process. This perspective is a large part of what distinguishes the growth planning process in this book from a more traditional "specialist as expert" approach.

An additional distinction of the process described in this book is the order in which we approach IEP development. It's an order that does, in fact, minimize some of the challenges teams normally encounter. The traditional way is to develop an IEP and then work to design specific interventions and measures. Unfortunately, this approach too often leads to goals that are not measurable and a plan that feels "owned" by the special educators and other specialists on the team, rather than owned by all. The approach in this book begins with the end in mind, as many in the field of education recommend. Team members work together to identify how to measure and how to support the student before finalizing each of the IEP's goals.

Student Stories

Carmen

Carter

Maggie

Danielle

In the pages ahead, I will introduce four students and use their stories to clarify the growth planning process for a variety of support and student profiles. These students and their experiences are amalgams of real students and their families, real profiles, and real challenges their support teams faced. Although these students are different in many ways, all are behind grade level on one or more critical skills and need targeted support. We'll follow the growth planning process for each, from the initial team meeting conducted to select the critical skills to target (which, for some, will feature annual IEP goals), to the means of measuring progress and using the data collected to inform instructional decisions.

Carmen's story will feature the most prominently. Threaded throughout the chapters, it will illustrate how to carry out each step of the growth planning process. I highlight her story because Carmen has a specific learning disability (a neurological learning difference), and specific learning disability is the most common category for which students qualify for special education services. Although the growth planning process applies widely to all students, the process for Carmen is one that almost all teachers can relate to and might embark on right away.

The appendixes provide additional examples of how teams carry out the individualized growth planning process for students at varying grade levels who need targeted support for a variety of reasons. You'll find the stories of growth planning for Carter, a 6th grader who has cerebral palsy and a cognitive difference; for Maggie, a 9th grader who has been diagnosed with autism spectrum disorder; and for Danielle, a 3rd grader who struggles with decoding and reading fluency. Again, although the examples in the book focus on students who are behind grade level on a skill, the process is useful for any individualized or personalized goal. Students do not need to be behind grade level to benefit from a growth plan.

Summary

Because the growth plan provides structure for designing individualized, inter-disciplinary support and measuring progress in the context of everyday class-room activities, it is a great fit for today's inclusive schools. Creating and using a growth plan ensures every student who needs support in critical skill areas—both those who qualify for special education services and those who do not—gets that support and makes progress toward meaningful goals. An IEP and growth plans can work together as separate but complementary documents.

Key Reminders:

- An IEP provides the broad-brush view of goals, services, and supports. Growth plans bridge the gap between an IEP and what teams of educators will do on a daily basis to support the student's development of identified critical skills.
- If a student has an IEP, growth plans should be created at the beginning of the IEP process by all members of the team, including the student's family, so that the finalized IEP is a solid, meaningful document.
- The growth plan is designed to support all students, and for many students, it will be the impetus to prevent school failure and the need for ongoing, intensive intervention.
- Although students who need intervention and support are the feature of this book, *any* student can benefit from having a growth plan that addresses their own interest-driven goals.

In the next chapter, we will explore the first step of the growth planning process —working together as an interdisciplinary team to identify critical skills that will become the foundation of the plan.

2

SELECTING CRITICAL SKILLS TO TARGET

The skills and behaviors a team selects to target form the foundation for the entire growth planning process. If we fail to focus on the goals that are the most important for the student's long-term success, the quality of the strategies and design of the plan are of little consequence. In this chapter, we will take on the important first step of the growth planning process: seeking team consensus on the most meaningful skills for the student to master during the year.

Context Matters

In an older paradigm of student support, it was the specialists who drove the determination of priority goals. Oftentimes, these priorities reflected the results of the standardized developmental or achievement measures. These were also the measures used to determine eligibility for special education services, and they were administered by school psychologists or specialists.

At first blush, this specialist-led process of identifying critical skills makes sense. After all, each of these specialists is the expert in his or her discipline and is the person best qualified to identify what the student needs to be able to do. And standardized instruments seem to be a sensible way to identify a student's greatest needs. However, as logical as this approach to selecting priorities seems, it misses so many factors that make each student an individual: his or her preferences, interests, motivators, classroom activities, routines, and performance relative to general curriculum standards.

Urie Bronfenbrenner (1977) remarked that "much of contemporary developmental psychology is the science of the strange behavior of children in strange situations with strange adults for the briefest possible periods of time" (p. 513). He was absolutely right. The items from standardized diagnostic instruments, administered in a vacuum to students who are unique individuals, should not be the primary means of determining goals that will drive growth plans or shape IEPs. Instead, teams must take a more comprehensive look at the student—the whole child—and consider far more than test scores. The goal is to target the skills that affect that particular student's ability to access the general curriculum and succeed in school and beyond. These are the *critical skills* that reach across the curriculum and across time.

Understanding the Student's Perspective

Before identifying these critical skills and discussing support needs, it is important that the team devotes time to celebrating the student's strengths and gaining deeper understanding of the student's interests, dreams, and priorities. That means getting the student's input—a 180-degree difference from setting goals based on test scores alone.

Students who are comfortable driving the IEP meeting should be invited to do so. Speaking in front of a team of adults may feel intimidating for other students, so teams will need to make decisions ahead of time about the best way to invite the student to share his or her experience. But all students must be part of rich conversations about their experience ahead of the meeting, and we must summarize and revisit their priorities during the meeting. No growth plan or IEP is meaningful if it does not honor the strengths, voice, and priorities of the student. This process of selecting skills should always feel like something that is being done *with* students, not *to* them.

The following six questions can help guide our discussions with students:

1. How do you enjoy spending time? What do you love to do?
2. In school, what is your favorite activity or time of day?
3. What do you feel are your strengths?
4. When do you feel successful and proud of yourself?
5. What would you like to be able to do better or more easily in school?
6. What kind of help do you think has worked for you? What kind of help doesn't work for you?

These questions are meant to provide general guidance, not a script to use with students. The questions should feel like natural, everyday conversational language, rather than an interview or protocol. Older students can also be asked about their dreams for the future and their plans after graduation. This part of the growth planning process is crucial if the plan is to truly be personalized with students and make a difference in their lives.

Guiding Questions for Identifying the Priority Skills

The person charged with facilitating the teaming process has the task of guiding the team to identify priorities for the growth plans. Again, the goal is not to identify every skill where a student needs support; it's about identifying priorities.

The following three questions should shape the team's discussion:

1. With which standards or skills expected at this grade level does the student need additional support or intervention?

2. What other critical skills or behaviors does the student need to better access the curriculum or participate more meaningfully in classroom activities and school routines?

3. Which of these skills and behaviors will have the greatest impact on the student's success and happiness, now and in the future?

Each person on the team has a role in answering these questions.

Academic Standards and Skills

Inquiry into the first question can begin with inviting the perspective of general education teachers, who brief the team on what students are expected to know and be able to do for the upcoming academic year. These teachers can also clarify what mastery of grade-level expectations looks like for the student's grade level. The discussion of standards and skills may involve review of the Common Core State Standards (National Governors Association [NGA] Center for Best Practices & Council of Chief State School Officers [CCSSO], 2010a, 2010b) or other standards used by the school, such as the C3 Framework for Social Studies State Standards (National Council for the Social Studies, 2013) or the Next Generation Science Standards (NGSS) (Achieve, 2013).

Specialists on the team can contribute by reviewing the student's progress data and leading a conversation about the student's performance on the grade-level expectations. For students who receive special education services, these data may be from the previous year's IEP goals, or the data may be a review of the student's recent performance in the classroom.

After the team has reviewed the student's skills relative to academic expectations for his or her grade level, it's time to ask which of these are critical skills. Again, the team should focus on the most important procedural knowledge for the student to master rather than on content knowledge that is isolated to a particular subject area at that grade level. For example, although the 6th grade social studies curriculum may include the topic of westward expansion, and a

6th grade student may need support to demonstrate competency with this topic, this is not something we would choose as a priority for a growth plan. As noted previously, *critical skills* are those that have an impact that reaches across subject areas and across grade levels. In this example, the critical skills team members might identify would be the ability to study events of the past and analyze problems; to apply knowledge to novel problems; or to take a position on a topic, develop a logical argument and rationale, and support the case with evidence.

When everyone on the team is involved in the conversation, complex patterns of skills and behaviors begin to emerge. Students may experience "motivation" or "engagement" differently with different people or in different contexts. Consequently, a student's behavior or skill expression can look different to different people, at different times of the day, or in different settings. The student's family, for example, might contribute insight into conditions or times of day during which the student finds it easier or more difficult to concentrate. Understanding a student's present level of performance as well as how the skill or behavior looks within general curriculum and home contexts is necessary to select goals that are meaningful.

Other Skills and Behaviors

Not every skill that students need can be found within the general curriculum standards. There are many skills and behaviors that students need to participate meaningfully in school routines, gain access to the general curriculum and learn, and have successful, happy lives. For example, students must be able to remain engaged with the curriculum and activities; communicate and collaborate with other students and adults; and organize their space, time, and materials throughout the day.

Skills in these areas can greatly affect a student's success, but frequently, even though parents or teachers may notice the student's struggle, these skills and behaviors do not make it onto a growth plan or IEP. Sometimes this is because the difficulty the student has is viewed as an inherent and unchangeable quality rather than a challenge that can be addressed through evidence-based support. Most of us have heard comments like "She is a student who has difficulty managing her time" or "He is a student who is always late with assignments."

But prerequisite skills and behaviors can, of course, be taught, and they are often as important to a student's success as mastery of any academic standard. Sometimes they are *more* important. As such, teaching these skills is a school's responsibility, and targeting them for growth is both sensible and correct.

The Number of Goals

There is no correct number of goals for growth planning or IEPs, but it is generally understood that adding more goals does not equal better outcomes for students. Instead, teams should select a reasonable number of goals that they agree are the most fundamental to the student's success across time. As schools begin the process of implementation, they may decide to begin with the achievable step of creating just one growth plan with each student.

A Common Challenge: Team Members Calling for Too Many Goals

Sometimes you'll find that team members want to continue adding goals to the IEP in order to be comprehensive. When parents advocate for additional goals, often it is because the IEP does not include goals for all of the student's needs. Although it may seem the right choice to try to create a comprehensive list of goals, the longer the list of goals, the more difficulty the team will have managing the implementation of strategies and coordination of data collection. Remember, this process is about intentional selection of skills to target. The student will still participate in the full curriculum.

continued

To Prevent or Respond to the Challenge:

• Remind the team ahead of time that the objective is to create interdisciplinary goals, not a set of discipline-specific goals to bring to the IEP meeting and then combine into an IEP. The interdisciplinary goals reflect the skills needed in general education settings.

• Reassure the family that the student will be supported in every curricular area. It may be that the parent has a specific priority in mind; families have the ability to see the "full picture" of their child, and their input must be valued. Often, though, the best response is to have the general education teacher explain how special skills that the parent is concerned about are taught and detail what plans are in place to provide all students with the appropriate differentiated instruction and support.

CARMEN'S STORY

 Carmen is a 10th grade student in a suburban school district who qualifies for special education under the category of specific learning disability. Carmen also has been identified as gifted. She was first referred for special education services in 2nd grade, when her family and teacher became concerned about her reading fluency and comprehension.

Although Carmen's rate of reading continues to be a bit slower than her peers, she is now reading text at and above grade level with high-level comprehension skills. When presenting her thoughts verbally, she performs at or above grade level in all subject areas, but writing remains an area of need. Although Carmen's writing expresses thoughts with maturity, and the individual sentences she writes are frequently clear, she has difficulty organizing her thoughts into paragraphs and producing whole papers that are clear and cohesive. She is also working to improve her skills in the conventions of writing; spelling, punctuation, and grammar are all a struggle for her. Carmen receives intervention targeting her writing within the general education classroom and in a learning support classroom for one hour each week.

The Team Meeting

Because Carmen has a diagnosis that makes her eligible for special education, her planning meeting was a formal IEP meeting. Both of her parents, her general education language arts teacher, her special education teacher, a special education facilitator, and Carmen were at the meeting.

In the meeting, Carmen's facilitator guided the planning conversation from a discussion of Carmen's current strengths and areas where she needed support to the selection priorities for her success in the general curriculum. All team members were a critical part of the conversation. The general and special education teachers presented data and work samples of Carmen's current writing skills. And Carmen's parents shared their observations, joys, and concerns. This collaborative conversation generated a set of critical skills that have real meaning to Carmen and will play a real role in both her immediate and future success.

After welcoming everyone, the special education facilitator, Kay, kicked off the conversation by asking Carmen's parents how they thought everything was going this year. Carmen's mom, Claire, explained that she was thrilled with Carmen's reading progress. "It's been such a delight to watch Carmen finally take off with reading," she said. "Carmen, tell everyone about some of your favorite books."

Carmen, who had developed an interest in nonfiction texts about historical female leaders, told the team, "I just finished a book about Rosa Parks that was so inspiring. I love reading about strong women in history and the impact they've had on our world." Everyone smiled at Carmen's enthusiasm. She'd really come into her own this year, exhibiting strong opinions and a new level of maturity.

Kay asked Carmen's special education teacher, Liz, to discuss Carmen's progress in literacy skills. Liz showed graphs of data and work samples, saying, "You can see how Carmen exceeded her goal from last year. She is now on grade level in reading comprehension!" Everyone agreed that the progress had been remarkable, and Carmen's parents were delighted to hear that she was finally on grade level in this area.

Her teachers, Liz and Masha, went on to describe Carmen's improved reading fluency, explaining that her pace had improved so much that Carmen was now comfortable reading for pleasure. Carmen beamed at the description of her effort and accomplishment. Kay turned to Carmen and asked, "You really enjoy reading now, don't you?" "Yes," Carmen replied with a smile.

Kay then asked the team to discuss the grade-level standards for 10th grade for which Carmen would require support. They focused on Carmen's writing skills. Her language arts teacher, Masha, began the discussion by sharing two pieces of Carmen's writing. She showed the group the graded papers' feedback and pointed out how, in both lengthy texts, the number of errors Carmen made in punctuation, capitalization, and spelling increased dramatically after the first few paragraphs. Carmen's dad, Jeremy, nodded and said, "I'm usually the one to help with that homework if she needs it, and I've noticed the same problem with errors in her social studies work." Special education teacher Liz added, "This seems to be what happens on all work that requires multiple paragraphs. For students like Carmen, who both have a learning difference and are gifted, it can be difficult to do the heavy thinking necessary to really engage in the task of expressing complex concepts and at the same time remember punctuation and spelling."

Here, Carmen interjected, "I know it should be easy to remember commas and periods, but for me, it's way harder to remember that stuff than it is to write a good paper. Grammar rules and spelling and stuff like that are so boring, too," she admitted, with a half-smile. Everyone laughed and agreed with her that it wasn't the most interesting skill to learn, but it was necessary to communicate her thoughts in a way that makes them easy for others to understand.

Next, Masha turned to the language arts skill of organization and clarity of writing: "I think we are ready to target skills that will help Carmen organize her writing. I'd really like to see her use a clear topic sentence, include lots of rich supporting detail for each paragraph, and organize it all clearly into a paper with headings." Again, sharing examples of Carmen's writing, Liz pointed out Carmen's pattern of moving abruptly from topic to topic without fully developing any of the details. To Carmen, she said, "When I give you the chance to talk aloud about your topic, you knock it out of the park! You express well-developed thoughts that are organized and supported by many rich details." The challenge, Liz added, was to transfer this skill into the realm of writing. She explained that she had ideas for teaching this skill and could work together with the language arts teacher and other general education teachers to support Carmen in this area.

After confirming with the team, including Carmen, that there were no other academic skill areas where she needed support, Kay asked them to consider other skills Carmen might need to support her success in the areas they'd identified. Carmen's dad, Jeremy, shared, "I'm worried that Carmen always has a lot of late or missing assignments." Carmen's mom, Claire, agreed, saying, "I know she wants to remember her homework, but she forgets to use the agenda and can't seem to get her work done on time." Carmen agreed, too. "Sometimes I do the homework but forget to take it back to school. Sometimes I even get it to school but forget to turn it in! I don't know why I can't remember," she added. "I think it's because I get totally involved in what I'm doing and forget about things that aren't related to that."

Masha said, "I usually tell the class as a group at the beginning of the class to turn in any homework assignments, but Carmen sometimes doesn't turn one in. I wasn't sure if you hadn't completed the assignment, Carmen, or if you had but still weren't looking for it. This helps me understand so much better. Let's figure out a way to help you remember."

Claire and Jeremy provided context and filled in some details. Carmen had a hard time remembering lots of things at home and a hard time keeping up with her things. Jeremy said, "I don't know if you all know this, but Carmen carries all of her textbooks in a backpack at school because she doesn't want to use the locker. She is afraid she'll forget something or forget the combination." Carmen looked embarrassed and didn't say anything. Her mother asked, "Is the forgetfulness related to her learning difference, or is this just something that happens with some teenagers?" Liz explained that many students with neurologically based learning differences have difficulty remembering to do things and keeping up with their materials—it is related to executive function, which many teenagers are still developing. "I can give you more information on executive function," Liz said to Carmen and her family, who agreed that they would like to learn more.

The team concluded this part of the IEP meeting—and growth planning process—by drafting the critical skills outlined in Figure 2.1.

FIGURE 2.1 CRITICAL SKILLS IDENTIFIED FOR CARMEN

1. Using correct punctuation, capitalization, and spelling throughout a multiple-paragraph paper.
2. Presenting a topic clearly in writing, using multiple supporting paragraphs, each with a topic sentence, supporting details, descriptive language, and headings.
3. Timely completion and submission of homework assignments.

Summary

This chapter outlined the process for identifying critical skills as a team—the first step of the planning process and the step that guides its overall direction. The collaborative dialogue at the center of this step is necessary to ensure that growth plans improve students' outcomes.

Key Reminders:

- The planning process should begin with a discussion with the student about his or her strengths, dreams, priorities, and needs. The student's voice should be clear and present throughout the process.
- In the planning process, teams should target skills that will impact a student's success in multiple areas of the curriculum and in the future. These are the critical skills.
- General education teachers must play a leading role in determining the critical skills teams select.
- Parents and families are the experts on their children. They have much of the information that is needed to truly individualize a student's plans.
- If a student is missing skills or behaviors that are needed for school success, even if these are not a part of the academic standards for the grade, the team must consider them critical skills that are as or more important than the academic standards.
- By prioritizing, the team can concentrate instruction and intervention efforts and measurement of progress on the skills that are most fundamental to the student's success.

In the next chapter, we will look more closely at the critical skills identified and consider the settings in which the team will deliver intervention and measure progress, focusing on connecting skills to the general curriculum and providing the appropriate support across contexts.

DETERMINING SETTINGS FOR INTERVENTION AND MEASUREMENT

3

For many teams, taking the time to determine the settings for support and assessment may be a new step in the planning process. Although teams creating IEPs may be accustomed to identifying the frequency of special services and even the location where these services will be delivered, determining the *settings* for support is different.

Any strategy the team chooses can and should be implemented by many people on the team and across multiple settings. For example, a special education teacher following an IEP might design a picture communication schedule for a student with autism and spend two hours per week using this strategy with the student in general classroom settings. During this time, the special education teacher would work with both the student and the classroom teacher to assess how the intervention is working and then collaborate on necessary adjustments. It's important to clarify, though, that these two hours would not be the only time the picture communication schedule would be used; it would be used in multiple settings—in every classroom and at home, too. The picture communication schedule is the *strategy*; the two hours per week with the special education teacher is the *service*.

Supporting Quality Instruction

Outlining the specific settings for intervention and support services and assessment is a way to make the school culture more inclusion-minded. Support and assessment of its effectiveness become an expected and seamless part of everyday classroom activities and routines—and it makes intervention more effective, too.

When team members share the assessment role, they can see, for example, that a student is progressing very quickly in language arts but not in social studies and explore possible explanations. By engaging in this interdisciplinary process of designing and implementing support and assessment for progress monitoring, all team members gain skills. The subsequent elevation in the quality of instruction and intervention benefits every student in the classroom.

Supporting Generalization

Explicitly identifying where to deliver support and monitor progress is an important part of helping students maintain and *generalize* the targeted skills—be able to use these skills across settings, among different people, and with different materials. Generalization is the fourth and final stage of skill development, which begins with *acquisition*, continues to *fluency*, shifts to *maintenance*, and then expands to *generalization* (Haring, Liberty, & White, 1978).

Have you ever learned how to do something long enough to get through a test and then completely forgot? We all have! In this case, your teacher measured only your acquisition of the skill. The first time students demonstrate a skill or knowledge, they show *acquisition*. Once students can perform the skill over and over consistently, they show *fluency* with the skill. When students show that they can keep using the skill beyond the instructional period, they have reached *maintenance*. And finally, when students can take the skills they've learned and use them across a variety of settings, they demonstrate *generalization*. *Generalization* is the term in the special education research that is equivalent to the concept of *transfer* of skills.

In reality, it matters little whether a student demonstrates a skill or a behavior in a separate setting with a specialist. The real concern is whether the student can use the skill in situations when it is authentically needed (Jung, Baird, Gomez, & Galyon-Keramidas, 2008). The members of Carmen's team wouldn't want her to use the correct conventions of writing only in language arts class; they want her to use this skill in all subject areas, when writing e-mails, on social media—all of which are authentic opportunities.

The experience of Norman Kunc, a well-known disability rights activist and presenter, underlines the importance of providing students with authentic opportunities to apply skills. Norman has cerebral palsy and reflects on his experiences as a student as he impresses upon audiences the need for all people to have an authentic sense of belonging. In an interview, Norman talked about "the stairs to nowhere"—a set of stairs that his in-school physical therapist required him to climb and descend, over and over (Giangreco, Cloninger, & Iverson, 1993). Norman was pulled out of his general education classroom and curriculum for this work. Were there no natural opportunities for Norman to practice his stair-climbing skills during the day? What about getting on and off the bus? What about walking into and around the school?

When we take students to a separate room to work on a skill without clear connection to how the skill should be used and supported throughout all relevant settings, we have led them up the stairs to nowhere. We make it more difficult for many of them to then use that skill in other settings, with other people, or with other materials. This is especially true for students who have cognitive differences. Determining exactly where we intend to systematically support the student and measure progress, then, is a necessary component of effective growth planning.

Choosing the Growth Plan's Specific Settings

Although intervention and support can be implemented in any setting, as relevant, the team chooses up to four settings (labeled as setting *a* through setting *d*) where they will measure the student's performance. These settings might be subject-area classes, times of day, areas of the classroom, classroom routines, or activities in which the student will use the priority skill or behavior.

Some skills and behaviors are needed in all settings, throughout the day. When this is case, the team decides when they want to measure progress. It's a perfectly valid choice to go with the settings in which assessment will be easiest. Or the team might select times of day when the student has the greatest difficulty with the skill or behavior. Or they could choose settings in which the student is showing the greatest success.

There is no one correct way for a team to choose the settings; they simply choose the ones that make the most sense for the student right now. The letters (*a–d*) that correspond to the settings are also found in the data map and will be discussed in Chapter 7.

More often than not, especially in middle and high school, subject areas serve as settings (see Figure 3.1). But there are many other options. Settings might be instructional arrangements within a classroom (e.g., individual, small-group, and large-group), an approach that is especially common for elementary students or for certain behavioral goals. Sometimes physical areas of the school (e.g., homeroom, cafeteria, playground, band room) serve as settings, particularly when goals relate to orientation, mobility, or behavior. In all settings, an adult in that setting—whether classroom or subject-area teacher, specialist, or classified staff member—is the one responsible for measuring the student's progress. Whenever possible, students can measure their own progress as well.

FIGURE 3.1 SUBJECT AREAS AS SETTINGS

Settings	
a	Mathematics
b	Language Arts
c	Science
d	Social Studies

The growth plan template featured in this book provides space for teams to identify up to four settings, but not every goal requires that many settings. The idea is for teams to select the number of settings that will provide a good representation of a student's performance in a natural environment. Note, too, that teams may find it necessary to change settings for a growth plan after it has been implemented for some time. This is especially relevant when students change grades or change schools. While it is perfectly acceptable to change settings, any time this is done, a new data map should be started so the setting for each data point remains clear.

A Common Challenge: General Educators Uncomfortable with Their Classroom Being an Intervention Setting

Because there is sometimes an assumption that intervention and progress monitoring of IEP goals is the domain of the special education teacher, general education teachers may be uneasy with the idea of having a setting attached to them and their classroom. It may be that they feel ill equipped to deliver intervention strategies and measure progress. Or they may feel that given everything else that is on their proverbial plate, intervention and progress monitoring is too much to ask of them.

continued

To Prevent or Respond to the Challenge:

• Reassure general educators that the progress monitoring piece of intervention and support takes only seconds—minutes at most—for each data point. The data they collect will be embedded within the natural classroom activities and assessments they already have planned.

• Ask general educators how often they feel they can commit to data collection. They may assume you are requesting daily data collection when all you need is data every other week. Establish achievable schedules up front to clarify the (minimum) time requirements.

• Consider having a special education teacher come and observe the student in the general education classroom to take data, or explore the feasibility of the specialist collecting a sample of existing student work from that setting to score and record data.

• Arrange for the general education teacher to work through the monitoring and data collection process with the specialist until he or she feels comfortable carrying out the process independently. We always want every task to be collaborative in nature so that everyone feels the workload has been distributed well enough that all tasks are manageable and coordinated.

CARMEN'S STORY

In determining the settings for Carmen's conventions of writing goal, the team identified her (a) language arts, (b) social studies, (c) science, and (d) film classes as settings for measuring her progress. The team selected these subject-area settings because they provide Carmen with the most writing opportunities. The settings portion of her growth plan is shown in Figure 3.2. (You can find Carmen's growth plan in its entirety in Chapter 7.)

FIGURE 3.2 SETTINGS FOR CARMEN'S CONVENTIONS OF WRITING GOAL

Settings	
a	Language Arts
b	Social Studies
c	Science
d	Film

Summary

This chapter introduced the task of selecting settings in which to measure progress. This step may be a new one for teams but provides the important context in which teams want to see students' skills develop.

Key Reminders:

• *Support* and *services* are not synonymous. *Services* describe the time a student spends with a specialist designing, implementing, or assessing intervention. *Support* refers to the specially designed strategies used to foster the student's efforts to master a critical behavior or skill. These support strategies can and should be implemented by many people on the team, not by the specialist alone.

• All members of the team share responsibility for monitoring and assessment. In this new paradigm, both support and assessment are a seamless part of everyday classroom activities and routines.

• By identifying where support will be delivered and where performance will be assessed, teams promote both generalization of skills and an inclusive school culture.

• Settings for growth plan implementation can be times of day, subject areas, routines, physical spaces in the school or classroom, or any other place or time that the team decides will be a beneficial environment for measuring the student's progress.

The next chapter will present the multiple ways we can measure performance and provide a framework for setting a scale for data collection.

4

OUTLINING INCREMENTS OF GROWTH

Once teams have determined the critical skills and the settings where intervention and assessment will occur, the next step is to determine how performance will be measured. To ensure each goal is truly measurable, teams need to take this step *before* the goals are made official.

Many special educators learned to write goals using the SMART acronym to make each goal *specific, measurable, attainable, relevant,* and *time limited.* Although this acronym can be useful in evaluating a goal's quality, I've learned an important lesson about SMART goals over the years: giving people a SMART acronym does not lead to SMART goals. When teams write a goal without first considering exactly how the skill or behavior will be measured, often the result is a goal that includes a number but cannot actually be measured. The better strategy is to outline the actual measure first, *then* write the goal.

Setting the Scale to Measure Performance

Typically, schools and districts allow teams flexibility in how they collect and present data on students' outcomes. Although flexibility in the method of measurement is important, it's essential that the data be presented in a way that all members of the team can understand. When everyone within a school or district agrees to use the same kind of scale when collecting and presenting data, individual teams need less time to unpack the data they gather and can devote more time to making sound, data-based decisions.

Goal attainment scaling is recommended practice for measuring student progress toward individualized goals (Cytrynbaum, Ginath, Birdwell, & Brandt, 1979; Ruble, McGrew, Toland, Dalrymple, & Jung, 2013).

I was first introduced to goal attainment scaling as a researcher. A colleague of mine, Lisa Ruble, and I received funding from the National Institutes of Health to study an intervention for students with autism (Ruble et al., 2013). One of our outcome measures was student progress on social, behavioral, and communication goals using goal attainment scaling. Through our work on this study, I realized that we should not be reserving this methodology for research; it should be a part of the daily work in every classroom when measuring growth on the many skills that we know matter most to students. Goal attainment scaling offers educators a way to communicate clearly both what is expected at any given time and at what level a student is performing on any learning or behavior goal (Jung, 2018). This method can be used for measuring progress on any individualized goal. Furthermore, students can learn this process and become increasingly active in developing their goals and measuring their own progress. What a wonderful opportunity to personalize learning and share ownership of the goal setting and assessment process with students. Although goal attainment scaling is best practice for measuring progress on individual goals, it's not how most teacher preparation programs teach data collection and progress monitoring.

Goal attainment scaling can be considered a ruler of sorts—one that can accommodate whatever measure makes the most sense for that goal. If a student wants to persist in reading longer, then "duration measured in minutes" may be the best measure. If a student wants to complete a certain type of task with less help, then "level of independence" may be the right choice. If the objective is to improve the quality of a skill's expression, we can use words to describe the characteristics of each step of that progression (Jung, 2018).

Using goal attainment scaling, teams develop individualized, leveled descriptions of progress for a student. Teams describe where the student is now in observable terms. Then they determine where they would like to see the student be at the end of a year, and describe this. Finally, they pick points between the baseline and the end goal and describe these increments of change. In most examples of goal attainment scaling, teams also pick a point above the goal and describe it too.

The scale included in the growth plan in this book is a modified form of goal attainment scaling. As seen in Figure 4.1, the scale comprises nine increments of progress. The 0 is baseline—where the student is when the goal is written. The 4 is the description of how the team expects the student to perform in one year. This level of performance is known as the "acquisition" criterion. The 1, 2, and 3 are the three increments of change between baseline and the goal; they serve as benchmarks.

There are nine increments on our modified goal attainment scale because there are nine months in the academic year. It's a setup that prompts teams to expect a measurable change in student performance each month. IDEIA requires that teams inform parents of students who receive special education services whether their children are on track to meet their annual goals. The only way we can answer this question is to have an expected rate of progress.

FIGURE 4.1 GROWTH PLAN SCALE

Scale		↗ ᴧ
Goal	**4**	
	3.5	
Benchmark 3	**3**	
	2.5	
Benchmark 2	**2**	
	1.5	
Benchmark 1	**1**	
	0.5	
Baseline	**0**	

Note that on this modified goal attainment scale, teams only define the five points on the scale attached to the whole numbers; it's a way of simplifying the scaling task. Teams then use the scale in the same way a person might respond to survey questions that use a Likert scale. On a Likert scale, there is often a description of some of the numbered points, while others are left with no description. The descriptions anchor the scale, and the unlabeled points allow for more nuanced distinctions of progress. When it is time to collect data, teams using the modified goal attainment scale choose the half numbers when the student's performance is between two of the descriptions. Goal attainment scaling gives teams the flexibility to use any type of measurement strategy they choose, the ability to collect and present data in the same way for all students and all goals, and a clear answer to whether a student is on track to meet annual goals.

Choosing the Measurement Method

Just because a goal includes a percentage or other number and *appears* to be measurable, there is no guarantee that it actually is measurable. In an effort to ensure the measurability of goals, some school districts have a policy that every goal has a criterion for mastery that is measured with a percentage, often 80 percent. Somewhere in recent history, we seem to have collectively decided that 80 percent equals mastery. But mastery of what, exactly? We have all taken tests that were difficult to pass and others where earning a perfect score was easy. The challenge is rooted in the inherent difficulty of the test, not in the percentage cutoff where pass turns to fail. Thus, 80 percent does not have any inherent meaning as "mastery." This concept is no different when applied to goals. But there's another problem with following a "percentage cutoff" policy: quite simply, percentage is often not the best way to measure progress. In fact, many times it is not even *possible* to measure performance using percentage.

Consider this goal: "During language arts, social studies, science, and film, Carmen will write using correct punctuation, capitalization, and spelling with 80-percent accuracy." This goal appears measurable, but is it? How would we meaningfully calculate the percentage of correct conventions of writing? Well, we might calculate the percentage of words spelled correctly, but it would be a tedious task. And how would we calculate the percentage of punctuation errors or of capitalization errors? For a goal related to mastering the conventions of writing, it makes much more sense, and is easier for everyone, to measure a *rate of errors.* The team may choose, for example, to calculate errors per numbers of words, sentences, paragraphs, or pages, depending on the student's baseline performance.

The bottom line is, when we try to force all goals to be measured with a percentage, we ignore many useful tools that are available to us. Flexibility in student measurement approaches benefits educators as well as students.

The Multiple Ways to Measure

Traditionally, collecting data to measure progress is seen as the responsibility of the specialists on the team. But unless a student is spending large portions of every day with a specialist, it is the general education teachers who have the most opportunities to see and evaluate the student's performance. Students also have many opportunities to reflect upon their own performance and use the goal attainment scale. Giving teams multiple ways to measure student progress is a better fit for reality, and it allows team members to choose an option that makes sense within all kinds of daily classroom activities. In this section, we will explore nine ways teams can measure performance when using modified goal attainment scaling: duration, frequency, latency, level of independence, rate, percentage, proportion, quality, and task analysis.

Duration

Duration data are collected by measuring the total time that a behavior is observed. It can be calculated precisely and to the second using a stopwatch, but more often within the context of a general education classroom, duration is estimated to the nearest minute or 5 minutes.

Teams should select duration when they want the student to demonstrate a behavior for a longer or shorter period of time (Cooper, Heron, & Heward, 2007). For example, measuring duration is useful when the goal is for the student to persist with a task, like independent reading, for longer amounts of time, or when the goal is for the student to refrain from an undesirable behavior. Figure 4.2 shows an example of a duration scale targeting task persistence.

Frequency

Frequency measures involve counting how many times a behavior or skill is observed during a particular classroom routine or set interval (Cooper et al., 2007). A team may, for example, determine that they want to see a student cite more pieces of evidence when making an argument or analyzing text in formal papers of three or more pages. The team members, then, would count the number of pieces of evidence the student cites within samples of work every time doing so is part of the assignment. Figure 4.3 shows a frequency scale measuring citation.

FIGURE 4.2 DURATION SCALE

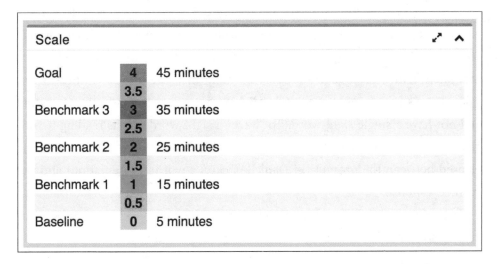

FIGURE 4.3 FREQUENCY SCALE

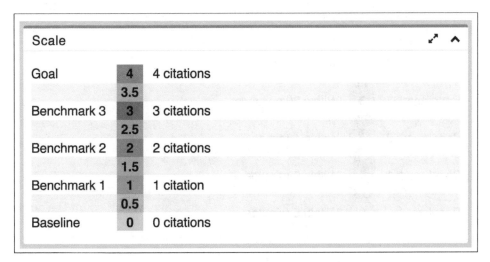

Latency

Latency is the measure to use when a team wants to see greater automaticity —demonstration of a behavior or skill more quickly after receiving a prompt. (Cooper et al., 2007).

Danielle is a student featured in the Appendixes. One of the critical skills Danielle's team chose is mastery of a greater number of sight words. Although it may seem logical to do this by keeping track of the number of words Danielle reads accurately, a measure of accuracy isn't the right measure of mastery here. Consider that a student might accurately read every word presented using decoding and not have a single sight word. To "have" a sight word means reading it with automaticity, not by decoding. We can measure latency by recording the time elapsed between the prompt (in Danielle's case, a word's presentation) and the correct response.

Latency is a good measurement choice for the common behavioral goal of getting started on tasks after directions are given, illustrated in Figure 4.4.

FIGURE 4.4 LATENCY SCALE

Scale			↗ ⌃
Goal	4	Immediately	
	3.5		
Benchmark 3	3	Within 30 seconds	
	2.5		
Benchmark 2	2	Within 1 minute	
	1.5		
Benchmark 1	1	Within 3 minutes	
	0.5		
Baseline	0	Within 5 minutes	

Level of Independence

One of the most meaningful ways team members can measure success is by recording the level of independence with which a student performs a skill. As the student gains independence with many skills across the curriculum, the team fades support. When fading support is part of the intervention strategy, level of independence is often the best way to measure progress.

Creating a level of independence scale requires the team to describe the various levels of assistance to be provided or independent action to be taken on the way to goal attainment. Because this scale does not depend on counting or calculating, teams must be precise with the language used to express the criteria, so that it is clear to everyone on the team how each level looks. Because level of independence scales include the prompts or supports that the team will use, team members must discuss and decide how they will teach the skill before writing the goal and the scale. Figure 4.5 shows a level of independence scale.

FIGURE 4.5 LEVEL OF INDEPENDENCE SCALE

Scale		
Goal	4	Independently, with or without checklist
	3.5	
Benchmark 3	3	With a checklist for proofreading and a reminder
	2.5	
Benchmark 2	2	With number/type of errors given, not marked
	1.5	
Benchmark 1	1	With location or errors marked, no correction
	0.5	
Baseline	0	With errors marked and correction given

It can be tempting to measure progress on this type of goal by using "number of prompts required." But is measuring whether a student needed four prompts or five really that useful? If it was necessary to repeat a prompt four or five times, then the prompt didn't work! It is better for teams to describe, in everyday language, the type of prompt the student may need and be specific about it. For example, the phase "a verbal prompt" may not provide team members with enough guidance. What *type* of verbal prompt? An explicit direction? A phrase? A leading question? See Chapter 6 for more information on prompt levels.

Proportion

Determining proportion is useful when a student has a variable number of opportunities to demonstrate a targeted skill or behavior (Cooper et al., 2007). Teams may use numbers to measure and report proportion (much as they might calculate a percentage), but they can also choose to use qualitative descriptions. Figure 4.6 shows a proportion scale expressed quantitatively, and Figure 4.7 shows a proportion scale expressed qualitatively.

FIGURE 4.6 PROPORTION SCALE USING NUMBERS

Scale		
Goal	4	9 of 9 steps
	3.5	
Benchmark 3	3	7 of 9 steps
	2.5	
Benchmark 2	2	5 of 9 steps
	1.5	
Benchmark 1	1	3 of 9 steps
	0.5	
Baseline	0	1 of 9 steps

FIGURE 4.7 PROPORTION SCALE USING WORDS

Scale		
Goal	**4**	All of the reading
	3.5	
Benchmark 3	**3**	Almost all of the reading
	2.5	
Benchmark 2	**2**	Most of the reading
	1.5	
Benchmark 1	**1**	Little of the reading
	0.5	
Baseline	**0**	None of the reading

Quality

Educators may believe that descriptions must include numbers in order to be truly measurable. As with the level of assistance, though, if the levels of performance are clearly described, the scale will be reliable even if nothing is being counted or calculated. Because classifying performance, rather than calculating it, is the real aim of goal attainment scaling, descriptions of quality are often the right choice for the scale.

Accordingly, when deciding how to measure the performance of a skill or behavior, it's better to describe what progress toward the goal looks like rather than trying to artificially assign numbers that can be calculated. Measures of quality allow teams to use narrative to describe increments of progress.

For teams, creating a quality scale is similar to writing a rubric. Figures 4.8 and 4.9 show two examples of quality scales: one to measure progress in the physical skill of writing and one to measure the behavioral goal of responding to a greeting.

FIGURE 4.8 ACADEMIC QUALITY SCALE

Scale		
Goal	4	Copies multiple complete letters legibly
	3.5	
Benchmark 3	3	Copies a complete letter legibly
	2.5	
Benchmark 2	2	Traces multiple complete letters
	1.5	
Benchmark 1	1	Traces a complete letter
	0.5	
Baseline	0	Copies a shape

FIGURE 4.9 BEHAVIORAL QUALITY SCALE

Scale		
Goal	4	Initiates greeting someone with a word
	3.5	
Benchmark 3	3	Initiates a greeting by waving and eye contact
	2.5	
Benchmark 2	2	Repeats a greeting with a word and eye contact
	1.5	
Benchmark 1	1	Waves when greeted and gives eye contact
	0.5	
Baseline	0	Uses no words or eye contact when greeted

Rate

Rate is a useful measure for time-based skills, such as reading pace or speed in solving math problems, in which the goal is to increase automaticity or fluency. The team member observes the student performing the skill for a set amount of time, records the number of errors made, and then calculates the rate of performance. When measuring reading pace, for example, this means dividing the number of words the student reads by the total number of minutes observed to calculate the rate in words per minute (Cooper et al., 2007). The rate scale in Figure 4.10 illustrates this example.

FIGURE 4.10 RATE SCALE FOR READING

Scale		
Goal	4	85 words per minute
	3.5	
Benchmark 3	3	70 words per minute
	2.5	
Benchmark 2	2	55 words per minute
	1.5	
Benchmark 1	1	40 words per minute
	0.5	
Baseline	0	25 words per minute

Time-based skills are not the only skills for which rate is a useful measure. It's also a good choice for a goal related to conventions of writing like the one Carmen has, where her team needs to measure the rate of her errors. Figure 4.11 shows a rate scale appropriate for that purpose.

FIGURE 4.11 RATE SCALE FOR WRITING

Scale		
Goal	4	1 error per 3 paragraphs
	3.5	
Benchmark 3	3	1 error per 2 paragraphs
	2.5	
Benchmark 2	2	1 error per paragraph
	1.5	
Benchmark 1	1	3 errors per paragraph
	0.5	
Baseline	0	5 or more errors per paragraph

Task Analysis

When a skill or behavior is easily broken into steps, and the goal is for a student to complete more of these steps, task analysis is likely the best measure (Cooper et al., 2007).

To measure using task analysis, the team first defines each of the task's steps and then collects data on which steps the student completes.

The goal set for Carmen to complete and submit homework is a skill her team can measure using task analysis. Figure 4.12 shows a task analysis scale they might use for this purpose.

FIGURE 4.12 TASK ANALYSIS SCALE

Scale		
Goal	4	Independently submits homework in class
	3.5	
Benchmark 3	3	Independently takes homework to school
	2.5	
Benchmark 2	2	Independently completes homework
	1.5	
Benchmark 1	1	Independently writes homework in agenda
	0.5	
Baseline	0	Needs prompt to write homework in agenda

Choosing the Right Criteria

When choosing criteria for the scale, teams must be sure to choose those that can be applied to a single event or observation. The scale will be used each time a team member needs to record data for a student's skill or behavior. If the scale includes words like "three times per week," then the scale cannot be used to record how the student performs on any given day. Ultimately, the data map (see Chapter 7) will show whether or not the student performed the task three times per week, but each data point must represent a single observation.

Ensuring Practical Criteria

Teams should phrase criteria in a way that reflects natural demonstration of the skill, rather than trial demonstrations. To suggest that the goal is for a student to "demonstrate a skill on six of eight trials" implies a testing situation in which the teacher provides eight trials. What is important is that the student can use the skill or behavior in authentic settings under authentic conditions.

The scales should be written in a way that allows measurement within these authentic contexts.

Ensuring Clear Criteria

Because multiple team members will be recording observations of the student's performance, the team must define each scale in a way that is not unnecessarily complicated and be sure that everyone understands how to use it the same way (Jung et al., 2008). The scale should ensure reliability among the people who use it—which means that two or more people could observe a student's performance (or review a student's work) and agree on the level of skill being demonstrated.

Ensuring Comparably Rigorous Criteria

In determining the highest level on the scale, teams decide the criterion they expect the student to reach by the end of a year. Teams must take care to be thoughtful in their choice so that they arrive at a statement of goal achievement that is both attainable and *comparably rigorous* to the general curriculum expectations. Yes, each scale's top-level criterion may be different from what is expected for this grade level, if that is necessary, but it should be comparably challenging for the student in question. If we are to move students forward toward grade-level expectations, we must aim high, and for this reason, their ending criteria should be in line with grade-level expectations as often as possible.

Another reason to embrace rigor is to ensure compliance with IDEIA for students who qualify for IEPs. In the U.S. Supreme Court case *Endrew F. v. Douglas County,* decided on March 22, 2017, the court unanimously sided with the family who did not believe the IEP created for their child was sufficient to ensure his adequate progress. The family had withdrawn their son from the public school and enrolled him in a private school for students with autism in an attempt to help him reach a new level of progress. The new school was able to demonstrate meaningful progress that his family argued he should have been able to make within the public school.

The court's ruling clarified that IDEIA intends for students to have more than minimum progress, and that a "child's IEP need not aim for grade-level advancement if that is not a reasonable prospect. But that child's educational program must be *appropriately ambitious* in light of his circumstances" (*Endrew F. v. Douglas County School District*, 2017).

The justices engaged in careful thought about the expectations educators should be setting and the language surrounding those expectations. Their written opinion reveals that they struggled with words like *appropriate, equal,* and the like, and were concerned that if they changed the expectation, it would prompt a burdening of the system with lawsuits. In the end, the court acknowledged that, while it's unreasonable to expect every student with a disability to achieve grade-level standards, educators should expect grade-level achievement when possible. And when we cannot expect grade-level achievement, we should offer a comparably challenging curriculum and expect student success within that curriculum (Jung, 2017a).

Given the unanimous ruling and precedent this decision sets, some schools are anxious to review their own policies, procedures, and tools to ensure they are meeting the legal requirements. The research indicates it's likely that many IEP goals are not measurable and not related to the general curriculum (e.g., Ruble, McGrew, Dalrymple, & Jung, 2010; Sanches-Ferreira, Lopes-dos-Santos, Alves, Santos, & Silveira-Maia, 2013). In fact, this is the area of the IDEIA with which states have historically struggled the most (Etscheidt, 2006).

To meet the requirements of IDEIA and satisfy the precedent set in *Endrew F. v. Douglas County School District,* it is imperative that teams work together to determine measures of student performance and ensure the criteria are comparably rigorous to those requirements students without disabilities have. Goals should not live from one IEP year to the next. Progress must be evident, and this progress should be evident in natural routines and settings, not only with a specialist or in a special education setting (Jung, 2017a).

A Common Challenge: The Scaling Task Feels Overwhelming

At this point in the process, teams may feel like defining the scale will be too much work and take too much time to complete during the IEP meeting. That feeling is understandable, as this undertaking likely represents a very different way of defining progress, and it requires the team to invest time in understanding multiple ways of measuring.

To Prevent or Respond to the Challenge:

• Explore alternatives to creating the scale during the IEP meeting. Perhaps a specialist and a general education teacher or two can begin thinking about the developmental progressions ahead of time, focusing on those that provide the easiest way to measure.

• Acknowledge that this is a new approach and that the team will need to invest time and thought to develop a solid measurement scale. Even though it represents more work at the outset, team members will be paid back ten-fold in how easy this process makes the subsequent tasks of progress monitoring and reporting. Once everyone has gotten the hang of writing scales, the work will not be as time-consuming or seem so tedious. And if the scales are written well, when it is time to send home progress notes, they can simply click "print" or copy the growth plans and notes.

Summary

This chapter presented the multiple ways we can measure student performance toward goal attainment and provided a framework for setting a scale for data collection.

Key Reminders:

- Goal attainment scaling is a method teams can use to create individualized scales that allow data to be collected and presented in the same way across goals and students.
- Including a number in the written goal does not guarantee the goal is measurable. Setting the scale before writing the goal ensures a measurable goal.
- There are multiple ways to measure progress. Teams should carefully choose the method that makes sense and is practical for use in the general education setting.
- Criteria for the scale should be comparably rigorous to the expectations of the general curriculum for the student's grade level. As often as possible, the goal should be to bring the student to grade level.

In the next chapter, we will look at how a team combines critical skills, settings, and scales to write measurable annual goals.

WRITING MEASURABLE GOALS

5

With a well-defined goal attainment scale in place, the next step for teams is to use the skill, settings, and scale to write measurable annual goals for the growth plan.

Although individualized outcomes are only legally required for students who qualify for special education services, *every* student who is behind grade level on a critical skill should have a growth plan with an annual goal. Arguably, every student at any level should have an annual goal and growth plan! Unfortunately, studies of the quality of individualized goals reveal what most families of students with learning differences already know: goals are often not specific, not measurable, and not relevant to general curriculum standards. The quality of goals declines further in upper grade divisions (Ruble et al., 2010; Sanches-Ferreira et al., 2013). Well-defined goals are needed to determine the strategies the team will use and to keep the entire team focused on and accountable to the agreed-upon purpose of support.

The Problem with Goal Banks

If we know what makes a measurable goal and can define many examples, then why not have a bank of goals from which teams choose? Wouldn't this ensure that every IEP, for example, has measurable goals and meets the requirements of the law? Plucking a goal from a list would certainly be quicker than convening a team to generate a scale of measurement for each student, as discussed in Chapter 4.

Although a goal bank may be a tempting option, defining *individualized* goals cannot work this way. Sure, we can identify common academic standards we would like students to achieve, but the reasons that students need support are diverse and numerous. And this diversity of strengths and baseline skill levels affects the goals we write. For example, we can identify based on grade level or course that we want students to solve a certain type of problem in mathematics. But if a student is having difficulty with this type of problem, before we can write a goal, we need to understand the nature of the student's difficulty. Is it difficulty understanding how to carry out the operations? Difficulty with math facts? Problems with checking work for errors of accuracy? Is the student having problems knowing which operations to use? Or is the student struggling to maintain engagement in difficult tasks? Without a clear understanding of the student's individual need, we *cannot* define the right goal for that student.

In addition to understanding the nature of the student's challenge with the skill, educators also need to understand exactly where the student is now and the student's current rate of growth. There is no one correct criterion for any skill. Defining the scale—including the criterion that reflects goal achievement —is all based on where a student is now, the trajectory of that student's growth, and how far we believe we can move the student's skills through appropriate intervention.

Each of these variables makes creating and drawing from a list of all possible goals impractical and unlikely to lead any team to select meaningful, individualized goals. This may be disappointing to teams that want to streamline the process and make goal writing more efficient. But if the goal selected is not the right goal for the student, there's no victory in wrapping up the planning meeting in record time. An easier process is not worth sacrificing the substance of the growth planning effort.

Refining Each Critical Skill

The formal goal writing gets under way with the team reviewing a critical skill or behavior they have chosen (see Chapter 2) and rewording it, as necessary, so that it is clear to all exactly what outcomes they are targeting (Jung, 2010; Sanches-Ferreira et al., 2013). For example, "Improve communication" is not as clear as "Use sentences of at least three words to make a request." "Improve writing" is not as clear as "Write paragraphs that are logically organized, clearly written, and related to a central topic."

When teams write growth plans to target a critical skill, there should be no room for misinterpretation. The result of this specificity may be a longer goal than teams are accustomed to seeing. It's true that simplicity has its advantages, but clarity is more important than brevity when writing a goal. Teams should use as many words as necessary to ensure everyone on the team fully understands the skill.

Choosing a Fluency Criterion

When delineating the points on the modified goal attainment scale, teams determined the *acquisition criterion* of each identified skill or behavior. This is the level to which the team expects the student to demonstrate the skill or behavior. For example, we might expect a student with a communication goal to take four turns in conversation or a student with a reading goal to read at a pace of 120 words per minute. The first time the student demonstrates the skill at that level, the student demonstrates acquisition. But we would not let go of the goal and call it complete the very first time a student meets that criterion.

Therefore, in addition to the acquisition criterion that was written for the "4" on the scale, teams should choose a *fluency criterion* for the goal. This criterion determines the amount of evidence the team requires to say that the goal has truly been met. For example, the team may want to see the student take four turns in conversation in 10 conversations within a single week. The 10 conversations within a week is the fluency criterion. A team may decide that the student's reading fluency goal should include reading at 120 words per minute on five one-minute samples of reading in a row. In this case, the five samples in a row is the fluency criterion.

The fluency criterion cannot be a part of the scale the team generates, because the scale must apply to a single observation. For this reason, only the acquisition criterion is on the goal attainment scale, but both the acquisition criterion and the fluency criterion are included in the goal.

Choosing the Wording

Once the team has determined the specific skill, chosen the settings, defined the increments of progress, and chosen the fluency criterion, they have everything they need to write an annual goal. There is no single correct way to word a goal, but the following structure is one that can help teams with the process of transitioning to measurable, interdisciplinary goals:

> [*preposition*] [*settings a, b, c, and d*], [*student name*] will [*critical skill or behavior*] [*acquisition criterion*] [*fluency criterion*].

For example:

> [During] [art, recess, morning meeting, and lunch] [Maggie] will [initiate a conversation] [with at least one peer in each setting] [for five days in a row].

After plugging the components into this structure, teams may decide to wordsmith the goal for improved clarity or conciseness.

A Common Challenge: Teams Prefer "the Old Way."

Teams usually have a routine for how goals are written. Sometimes there are even policies in or forms in place that force a different way of writing goals. Team members may find the new way too wordy and prefer phrasing that is "less specific."

To Prevent or Respond to the Challenge:

• Remind team members of the criticality of this work—how essential it is to have clear and measurable goals, the school's obligation to ensure adequate progress (affirmed in *Endrew F. v. Douglas County*), and the purpose of goal setting, which is to determine the most important academic and behavioral goals a student needs to be successful in life. This is a really important task!

• Help to make the process easier by walking team members through the components of the template ahead of time.

• Remember that time invested now to write clear, meaningful, and measurable goals means team members will be able to show when student progress is on track—and make adjustments when it is not.

CARMEN'S STORY

After discussing Carmen's priorities for the year, the team determined the best places to measure progress on each goal. They confirmed that even though various team members could implement intervention outside the general education classroom, each of Carmen's targeted outcomes would be measured most authentically by scoring her progress within the context of her general curriculum assignments. Figures 5.1, 5.2, and 5.3 show the three goals that Carmen's team chose for her.

FIGURE 5.1 CARMEN'S CONVENTIONS OF WRITING GOAL

		Annual Goal
Critical skill	Write paragraphs with correct punctuation, capitalization, and spelling.	In language arts, social studies, science, and film, Carmen will write paragraphs with no more than three punctuation, spelling, or capitalization errors for every five paragraphs on 10 pieces of writing.
Settings	Language arts, social studies, science, and film	
Acquisition criterion	No more than three errors per five paragraphs	
Fluency criterion	On 10 writing assignments	

FIGURE 5.2 CARMEN'S PARAGRAPH WRITING GOAL

		Annual Goal
Critical skill	Write five paragraphs with these six components: an introduction, three supporting details in each paragraph, a variety of descriptive words and phrases to add depth, and appropriate citations.	On writing assignments of five paragraphs or more in language arts, social studies, and film, Carmen will use an introduction, at least three supporting details in each paragraph, a variety of descriptive words and phrases that add depth, and appropriate citations on 10 assignments in a row.
Settings	Language arts, social studies, and film	
Acquisition criterion	All six components	
Fluency criterion	On 10 writing assignments	

FIGURE 5.3 CARMEN'S HOMEWORK COMPLETION GOAL

		Annual Goal
Critical skill	Complete and submit homework.	In language arts, mathematics, science, and social studies, Carmen will consistently complete all five steps of submitting complete and timely homework, with no more than one late assignment per month.
Settings	Language arts, mathematics, science, and social studies	
Acquisition criterion	All five steps, independently	
Fluency criterion	No more than one late or missing assignment per month	

Summary

This chapter outlined the way that teams put together the skill, settings, and criteria to write an individualized, measurable goal for students. The resulting goals are interdisciplinary—they include the contributions and support of every member of the team. Each goal is applicable to many settings and written to ensure general educators in those settings can implement interventions and assess student progress.

Key Reminders:

• Writing individualized goals that are measurable requires teams to first select the skill, settings, and criteria.
• Although a goal bank is a tempting solution to the challenge of providing goals that are measurable, it compromises the individualized nature of growth planning. There is no real shortcut to the process.

- An acquisition criterion is the level at which the team wants to see the skill at the end of a year. The fluency criterion is the amount of evidence the team needs to see to judge the goal as being complete. Acquisition criteria are included in the scale, but fluency criteria are only included in the goal.
- One useful format for writing measurable goals is as follows: [*preposition*] [*settings a, b, c, and d*], [*student name*] will [*critical skill or behavior*] [*acquisition criterion*] [*fluency criterion*].

The next chapter moves into planning the interdisciplinary strategies that will support students across the curriculum. This is the part of the planning process in which teams determine what everyone on the team will do during daily routines and activities to help the student make progress toward the goal.

6

DEVELOPING INTERDISCIPLINARY STRATEGIES

With a clear direction in place in the form of measurable goals, teams can turn to determining how to support the student's progress toward those goals. In the past, the work of selecting strategies was typically taken on by the specialist or special educator, who might also have been the only person to implement the chosen strategies. We now know that this is not the best approach to support learning or promote inclusion.

The Value of a Systematic Interdisciplinary Approach

As teams convene to develop the strategies for a student, it is necessary that the process remains interdisciplinary; all team members must agree that neither strategy development nor implementation will be the responsibility of a single person or discipline. The strategies teams develop should arise from the experiences and ideas from everyone on the team and form a cohesive, interdisciplinary plan uniquely designed to meet an individual student's needs.

Let's take a step back. Naturally, we tend to think of specialists as being the experts on certain skills or portions of the curriculum. An occupational therapist, for example, is the expert on fine motor skills and sensory issues. Similarly, the reading specialist is the expert on reading support. The behavior specialist is apt to have the best ideas on how to support any given behavior change.

Although this expertise on skills or behaviors does, indeed, belong to people who have undergone extensive training and perhaps licensure in these areas, this does not mean these specialists should design support strategies in isolation from the team. Certainly, selecting the best strategies requires the expertise of those who best understand the applicable research and have the requisite training on the associated skills, but developing these strategies also requires the participation of the people who know the student the best and the people who know the curriculum the best. As a part of developing support strategies, teams must think about how the strategies will be individualized for the student and delivered within the context of classroom routines and activities.

When combining their expertise and experience in an interdisciplinary team, every member must think creatively. *Developing solid support strategies is as much an exercise in problem solving as it is having the right menu of strategies at your disposal.* The occupational therapist may have watched a general education teacher use a behavioral strategy with a student last week that was incredibly effective; it might be a great strategy for the team to discuss at this IEP or intervention planning meeting. The fact that it was not a part of the occupational therapist's original training is no reason not to discuss it as a possibility. A father may have a great idea he gained from interacting with his child at home. The parents at the table will almost always have ideas that come from their wealth of experiences and "homegrown data." The intersection of these perspectives, experiences, and expertise is where the most meaningful strategies are born.

Strategies to Consider

With seemingly infinite choices of support strategies and programs, deciding where to start can sometimes be overwhelming. The next several pages present the most common evidence-based academic and behavioral strategies, all of which can be used in general education settings.

Common Academic Intervention Strategies

Dialogic reading is a strategy that supports improved reading comprehension skills and language skills. With dialogic reading, the teacher pauses periodically while reading aloud and engages the student in a short discussion of the text. The discussion includes prompts and questions that allow the teacher to gain an understanding of the student's comprehension, build the student's comprehension by clarifying and elaborating, and grow the student's vocabulary The interaction of dialogic reading can also improve student engagement (Morgan & Meier, 2008; Whitehurst, Epstein, Angel, Payne, & Al, 1994). *Learn more online:* National Center for Learning Disabilities.

Direct instruction (DI) is a method for teaching mathematics and literacy skills that uses prescriptive lessons designed to teach small increments of skills and build toward mastery over time. The scripted approach, in which all material is presented in the same way each time, allows the student to focus cognitive energy on the new concept rather than on interpreting the teacher's prompts. Each increment of learning is followed by student practice, and the teacher immediately corrects any error and reinforces student engagement (Adams & Carnine, 2003; Engelmann & Bruner, 1969; Rupley, Blair, & Nichols, 2009). *Learn more online:* National Institute for Direct Instruction.

Expansions are used to increase a student's vocabulary and improve grammar and word usage. With expansions, the adult restates what the student said using the student's words and including new vocabulary or a more complex sentence structure, or making a correction. For example, if a student says, "The three authors had really different ways of saying the same things," the adult might expand this to "Yes, the authors presented the same topic in contrasting ways, which was particularly apparent in their use of voice and sensory language." Expansions are helpful for students with language-based learning differences, students who are English learners, and students who need support building vocabulary (Mackey & Philp, 1998). *Learn more online:* American Speech-Language-Hearing Association; search for "expansions."

Feedback is the information a teacher gives students to describe their progress toward a goal and what they should do next to get there. Feedback is a powerful tool and should be a part of the informal and formal formative assessment conducted on a daily basis with all students. Feedback should begin with the positive, be specific, and be delivered during or immediately following the assessment (Moss & Brookhart, 2009). *Learn more online:* Edutopia; search for "feedback."

Graphic organizers are visual representations of informational relationships and patterns. Venn diagrams, flowcharts, webs, maps, and process charts are examples. Because graphic organizers make the relationships and patterns within information explicit, the student is able to focus on understanding the information rather than on working to understand how it's organized. The visual also boosts some students' abilities to recall the information (Meyen, Vergason, & Whelan, 1996). *Learn more online:* Freeology.

Mnemonics pair information the student knows well or can easily remember with more complex information to help the student remember the complex information. Rhymes, acronyms, pictures, or movement can all be used as mnemonics to help recall information (Wolgemuth, Cobb, & Alwell, 2008). Mnemonics are excellent resources for students who have learning differences and cognitive differences, but they are useful for all students needing to remember complex information. *Learn more online:* LD Online; search for "mnemonics."

Peer-Assisted Learning Strategies (PALS) is a program in which students who are having difficulty with a skill or concept are strategically paired with a peer coach who has mastered the skill or concept. Pairs throughout the classroom work simultaneously, sometimes all on the same skill, and sometimes on different skills. Pairs are not static, and all students serve as a coach at some point over a set period of time. Teachers move about the room to provide assistance and feedback during paired activities (Fuchs et al., 2001; Fuchs, Fuchs, & Burish, 2000; Fuchs, Fuchs, & Kazdan, 1999; Fuchs, Fuchs, Mathes, & Simmons, 1997). *Learn more online:* Vanderbilt Kennedy Center; search for "PALS."

Common Behavioral Intervention Strategies

Chaining is a strategy in which the behavior is broken down into small steps through task analysis. Each small step of the behavior is taught one at a time. By mastering small chunks of the skill or behavior, the student is able to learn complex or multistep skills. In forward chaining, the student is taught the first step in the instructional sequence first. In backward chaining, the last step is taught first (Alberto & Troutman, 1999; Cooper et al., 2007; Cox & Boren, 1965). *Learn more online:* Indiana Resource Center for Autism; search for "chaining."

Differential reinforcement of other behaviors (DRO) involves reinforcing any behavior that is not the one the team wants to decrease. For example, if the team wants to eliminate the behavior of being disengaged, a teacher may smile and compliment a student for working with a group to research a topic in science. The focus is on reinforcing the student's positive behavior rather than exclusively correcting the negative behavior (Shabani, Wilder, & Flood, 2001). *Learn more online:* Applied Behavioral Strategies.

Extinction of challenging behaviors involves removing whatever is reinforcing the behavior that the team want to eliminate. Every team member has to implement this strategy in the same way for it to work. When implementing extinction, it's common for the undesired behavior to temporarily increase, but if everyone sticks with the strategy, then the behavior will decrease and eventually be eliminated. Extinction leads to a relatively permanent change in behavior. Teams should pair extinction with reinforcement of a replacement behavior (Iwata, Pace, Cowdery, & Miltenberger, 1994). *Learn more online:* LD Online; search for "extinction."

Functional assessment of behavior (FBA) is the first step teams should use to determine how to intervene when a challenging behavior is not responding to typical classroom behavior management practice. Through FBA, a team member observes the student when the challenging behavior is likely to occur. The observer records what happens just before the behavior (antecedent), during the behavior, and just after the behavior (consequence). After the observation, team members examine the sequence of antecedents, behaviors, and consequences to determine why the behavior is occurring and being maintained. With information on what is serving as the reinforcer for the student, the team can design a growth plan to replace the challenging behavior with a new, desirable behavior (Cooper et al., 2007; Watson & Steege, 2003). *Learn more online:* Center for Parent Information and Resources.

Limited choice making prevents problem behaviors by providing the student with several appropriate choices. In this way, educators ensure that the student demonstrates the skill or behavior the team wants to support while maintaining some choice within defined parameters. For example, a student may be allowed to choose a book from a selection of books to read and write about. Or a student may choose among several different but defined writing assignments to demonstrate writing skill. Young students with challenging behaviors benefit greatly from limited choice making, especially when the choice is emphasized and used as a way to decrease the focus on what the student does not want to do. For example, a student who displays physically aggressive behavior when it is time to go from art class to lunch can be given any number of choices, such as whether to lead the line, turn off the lights, or decide which hat to wear. The one choice that isn't available is whether to go from the art classroom to the lunchroom—the target behavior (Cordova & Lepper, 1996). *Learn more online: Alfie Kohn; search for "choice making."*

Picture Exchange Communication System (PECS) was developed as a communication intervention for individuals with autism spectrum disorders. PECS is an evidence-based practice for individuals of all ages with a variety of communicative, cognitive, and physical difficulties that uses pictures as symbols to represent all parts of speech. For students who lack the verbal skills to communicate, teachers use PECS to teach the student to give a picture of a desired item to an adult or peer, who immediately honors the request. PECS can be used to teach discrimination of pictures, how to put them together in sentences, and how to use pictures to answer a question or comment. For students who are able to use many pictures, pictorial sentences and responses can be assembled in a book. Other students may transition to electronic platforms, such as an iPad, for using PECS. Many students who learn to communicate with PECS also develop speech. Others may transition to a voice output system for communication (Bondy & Frost, 1994; Hart & Banda, 2010). *Learn more online:* PECS-USA.

Social stories are personalized stories with text and visuals that script a desired behavior for a student. Social stories are used frequently with students with autism but are also useful for young students and those who have cognitive differences. An adult or peer reads the social story with the student, after which words from the story are used when intervening with the behavior when an opportunity occurs (Gray, 1993). *Learn more online:* Carol Gray Social Stories.

Shaping involves reinforcing successive approximations of the desired response. That is, the student is required to improve the quality of his or her response more and more to receive the reinforcement. For example, a student who has difficulty remaining engaged in classroom activities may initially be reinforced for remaining in the correct location. After the student demonstrates this behavior for a period of time, the reinforcement may be delivered after the student remains in the correct location and is focused on the activity for several minutes. In this example's final stage of implementation, the reinforcement is delivered only when the student remains in the location, is focused on the activity, and completes the activity (Alberto & Troutman, 2003). *Learn more online:* Nebraska Autism Spectrum Disorders Network; search for "shaping."

Strategy instruction is an intervention in which a student is explicitly taught an effective approach to a skill or behavior. This is different from teaching a student the content; it's a method for teaching skills and behaviors that allow the student to access the content. Examples include teaching specific strategies for taking notes, studying, interacting with classmates, managing time and materials, and regulating emotion (Ellis, 1994; Spörer, Brunstein, & Kieschke, 2009; Weinstein & Mayer, 1986). *Learn more online:* Parent Center Hub.

Keeping Up with the Profession

But these strategies, which many of us learned in our teacher or personnel preparation programs in college, are only a beginning. The best way to stay abreast of evidence-based strategies is for all team members to follow the research of their disciplines. Many team members will find that membership in Council for Exceptional Children (CEC) and its associated divisions meet this need. Visit cec-sped.org for more information.

For extensive information on more instructional strategies and their effectiveness, consult the What Works Clearinghouse (https://ies.ed.gov/ncee/wwc). Teams may find the "Educator's Practice Guides" within the clearinghouse to be particularly useful, as it is searchable by topic. For example, an educator could select "literacy" and, within the practice guides, select "Teaching Elementary School Students to Be Effective Writers." Within that practice guide are four recommendations, each with clear implementation steps. These research-based practice guides can be an efficient tool for teams to consider as they develop interdisciplinary strategies.

Building one another's basic knowledge of the most common interventions that can be used in the general education classroom allows everyone on the team to play an active role in crafting a plan for support and use a wider variety of tools. General education teachers have the chance to learn some of the strategies the specialists use, and specialists gain a deeper understanding of the curriculum and strategies general educators use. What a powerful combination! Now we have the makings of an effective team.

Behavioral Supports for Academic Goals

Behavioral strategies are not just useful for students with identified behavioral needs. Any student who needs support for academic goals benefits from behavioral strategies, for several reasons. First, academic and behavioral needs often overlap, and supporting positive behaviors during academic intervention is a wise investment for educators to make with any student. Second, everyone enjoys doing those activities that we feel good or talented at doing, and most of us find it difficult to keep trying when we feel we are not good at the task. When students are struggling with an academic skill, it is imperative that we not only acknowledge the academic progress they make but also support and develop the effort and perseverance they are showing.

The Language of Behavioral Support

To be systematic about our support of students' behavior, it helps to establish common language around these strategies. Although the strategies for supporting students' behaviors are largely centered on reinforcing what educators want to see, an understanding of both reinforcements and punishments, and of both positive and negative strategies, can be helpful as teams design their approach. Figure 6.1 provides a framework for the vocabulary of reinforcements and punishments.

Many people mistakenly use the term *negative reinforcement* to mean a student is being punished in some way—that he or she is experiencing a negative consequence. *True* negative reinforcement, as clarified in Figure 6.1, means taking away something in an effort to increase instances of a behavior. Essentially, we remove something a student does not value (such as homework) to

FIGURE 6.1 OVERVIEW OF REINFORCEMENT AND PUNISHMENT

	Reinforcement	Punishment
Positive	Adds something to increase a behavior *Example:* Giving a student a compliment and a smile for working hard.	Adds something to decrease a behavior *Example:* Giving a student detention for repeatedly talking out of turn.
Negative	Takes away something to increase a behavior *Example:* Taking away homework for a student who persisted at a difficult task.	Takes away something to decrease a behavior *Example:* Refusing to acknowledge a student when he or she speaks disrespectfully.

encourage behavior we want to see. In this context, *negative* means "to take away"; it has nothing to do with how the action feels to the student. Similarly, *positive* means "to add something." A positive reinforcement, then, means the team has added something the student values (such as praise) in order to increase expressions of a behavior they want to see. Teams do best to focus on the left side of Figure 6.1's table and provide positive and negative reinforcement of behaviors they want to see much more often than they use punishments to decrease a behavior they don't want to see. Positive punishments should be the strategy used least frequently.

Reinforcement Schedules

Reinforcement schedules are the planned times that reinforcements are delivered (Alberto & Troutman, 2003). There are several schedules of reinforcement that teams can use to promote the behaviors they want to increase in the classroom. Here are three to consider, from most intensive to least intensive.

- *Continuous reinforcement.* With this schedule, reinforcement is given to the student every time the student shows the desired behavior or skill. Continuous reinforcement is most useful when students are first learning a new skill or behavior.
- *Fixed ratio or interval reinforcement.* In this schedule, the reinforcement is given after a predetermined amount of time or number of times the desired behavior or skill is witnessed. This is the schedule teams choose when a student has demonstrated acquisition of the skill or behavior and they want to fade support.
- *Intermittent reinforcement.* With this schedule, reinforcement is delivered at varied times so that students are unable to predict when the reinforcement might happen. Once a skill or behavior is learned, this is the most powerful schedule for maintaining that behavior. (Intermittent reinforcement helps to explain why some people become addicted to gambling; the person never knows when the reinforcement is going to be delivered and persists in the behavior because the payoff could come at any time.) Intermittent reinforcement should be a part of the core instruction in all classrooms.

Levels of Prompting

Prompts are intentional signals delivered to increase the likelihood that students will make correct responses (McClannahan & Krantz, 2010). Teams should agree on a systematic approach to using prompts to help students learn skills and acquire behaviors.

Because student independence is the endgame, it's important to use the least intrusive prompts that will allow the student to be successful. Figure 6.2 lists common prompt types, from most to least intrusive.

FIGURE 6.2 PROMPT HIERARCHY

Prompt	Description	Example
Full physical assistance	Physically support student throughout the entire skill task	Holding a student's hand to walk between classes
Verbal direction	Use words to direct the student in what to do	Telling a student to put items away and transition to the next activity
Verbal hint	Use words, often questions, to prompt the student to remember what to do next	Asking a student what the next step is in writing a paragraph
Partial physical prompt	Intervene physically to guide part, but not all, of a task	Giving a gentle touch to a student's shoulder to remain engaged without using any words
Gesture	Use facial expressions, body movements, or positions to support the student	Shrugging shoulders with hands extended to ask a student, "What's next?"
Auditory prompt	Use a mechanical sound (e.g., chimes, bell, whistle, claps, song) instead of a person's voice to prompt a response	Using clapping rhythms to secure students' attention
Textual prompt	Use written words, lists, and other text to support a student	Using a checklist that includes the steps of writing to support a student with a writing task

Individualizing the Support Strategies

Simply selecting a support strategy to use for a student is not enough. Teams must also consider the ways that the strategy should be customized for that individual student. This means accounting for the student's interests, preferences, dislikes, and so forth and meaningfully individualizing each strategy (Jung, 2017c). Teams should also discuss the characteristics of the settings where intervention will be delivered, where the natural learning opportunities lie, and how the strategies might best be deployed in those settings.

The Importance of Fading Support

Regardless of the supports teams select to provide a student with access, it is important that they consider how they will fade the support—systematically and gradually reduce it over time in order to build independence to the greatest extent possible (Neitzel, 2009). A team may, for example, determine that a student needs an adult to be nearby and able to provide prompts so that the student will remain engaged in seat work. Providing this level of support ensures the student's access to the instruction and practice. However, the end goal is that the student can remain engaged *and* do so independently. The only way to reach that goal is to systematically provide less and less support, helping the student to make small, incremental steps toward independence.

Strategy Use Throughout the Day

In addition to planning the times for support to be delivered, the team should plan for other teachable moments during which the selected strategies can be used. This is a way for students to receive more instruction and targeted support in contexts that are meaningful to the student. The instruction, then, is immediately relevant. For example, the team may have developed a growth plan to support a student's ability to use all mathematical operations with decimals. The support is planned for math and science class, where the curricula involve explicit instruction within activities and lessons. But when else might the student need to employ the targeted skill, giving rise to a teachable moment? The team might identify "when buying lunch in the cafeteria" or "when making a purchase at the mall." With these situations identified, team members, including family members, will be better prepared to use incidental teaching within these contexts, helping the student to generalize the skill.

Adaptation Strategies

As teams make decisions about strategies to use, it is important to note which ones constitute accommodations and which are modifications. The difference between these two categories of adaptations has important implications for instruction, intervention, and assessment. Let's take a closer look.

Accommodations

Accommodations are adaptations that provide access to the general curriculum but do not fundamentally alter the learning goal or grade-level standard. These supports "level the playing field" (Freedman, 2005, p. 47). Within the context of assessment, accommodations are *support for a skill that is different from the skill being measured.* Take, for example, a driver's exam. The skill being measured is driving. For this reason, support of a person's vision with glasses or contact lenses is an allowed accommodation. A person who needs glasses definitely finds driving easier *with* glasses than without them. But once the street signs, lines on the road, and other vehicles are visible to the glasses-wearer, all the challenges specific to driving remain. The accommodation doesn't make driving easier for the glasses-wearer than it is for a non-glasses-wearer; it simply levels the playing field. There is support for vision, but we are measuring driving.

Now let's take an academic example: a social studies assessment. The purpose of the assessment is to determine the student's level of mastery on a number of social studies standards. Support of any skill or behavior that is not related to the social studies standards is an accommodation. We may permit a student to respond orally if significant issues related to the student's writing affect the quality of response. We may allot additional time or provide a separate testing environment if test anxiety is a factor. An adult might read the questions to the student if there is difficulty with reading. Each of these adaptations is an accommodation, because each one supports a skill that is different from the social studies standards being measured and reported (Jung, 2017c).

Modifications

Modifications are changes to the curriculum and assessments that do fundamentally alter the learning goal or grade-level expectation. Unlike accommodations that simply level the playing field, modifications "change the game" (Freedman, 2005, p. 48). We have made a modification to an assessment when we *support the skill that is being measured*. Returning to the vision example earlier, if a person wears glasses or contact lenses during an eye exam, it's an action that changes what the exam is measuring: the exam is not assessing the person's natural visual acuity but the effectiveness of the corrective lenses being worn.

Next, consider a mathematics example. Students in the class are working on algebraic problems that require multiplication of fractions. One student who needs support is working below grade level in math and is learning multiplication with whole numbers. This student's assessment does *not* include the grade-level algebraic problems that require multiplication of fractions. Instead, it includes whole-number multiplication problems and one-step algebra problems requiring addition and subtraction. The student's team determined this is the appropriate change to be made, a skill that is comparably rigorous for this student. Still, what is being measured has been changed. The math skill being measured is the skill that is being supported, and the support is a modification (Jung, 2017c).

Choosing the Right Adaptation

When teachers provide accommodations and modifications, they differentiate to give each student the support necessary to make progress. Figure 6.3 provides some examples. Modifications are more significant support, but this is not saying they shouldn't be used. If a student is significantly below grade level, for any reason, modifications and a growth plan are likely necessary.

Accommodations play an important role in ensuring we actually measure what we intend to measure. If a student fails to perform well because of anxiety about being timed, we cannot say the student did not understand the content. We must, to the greatest extent, remove the anxiety that prevents accurate measurement by providing extended time that allows us to get valid information about what the student knows.

This same principle applies to all students, not just to those who have IEPs. If *for any reason* we, as teachers, have evidence to believe there is an external influence affecting how a student performs on the skill we are measuring, it is our responsibility to reduce or eliminate that influence. What makes the influence external? Difficulty with any skill other than the one explicitly being measured with this task. Being able to clearly distinguish accommodations from modifications ensures we can always make accommodations available to any student who needs them (Jung, 2017c).

On Grade Retention

Repeat after me: Retention is not an intervention. Retention is not an intervention. *Retention is NOT an intervention!* It is imperative that all school faculty and administrators understand this. If something did not work the first time, providing more of the same is not the answer (Jung, 2017d).

FIGURE 6.3 EXAMPLES OF ADAPTATIONS AS ACCOMMODATIONS AND MODIFICATIONS

Adaptation	Accommodation	Modification
Extended time	Any time rate or speed is not the skill being measured. This is almost always the case. *Example: Measures of science or art knowledge*	When rate or speed is fundamental to the skill being measured. *Example: Measures of reading or math fluency*
Completing task orally	When that writing is not the skill being measured and reported. *Example: A research paper in science*	Any time writing skills are being measured and reported. *Example: An essay in language arts*
Fewer questions	As long as all questions measure the same skill and are of comparable difficulty, taking away some questions only shortens the assessment. It does not make it easier. *Example: Removing half of the 2-digit division problems on a math task*	Taking away the harder questions or omitting one of the skills measured. *Example: Removing the higher-level analysis essay questions and leaving the recall questions*
Prompts and cues	When the prompts and cues support a skill other than the skill being measured and reported. *Example: A graphic organizer to support a student's writing skills on a paper designed to measure skills in social studies*	Any time the prompts and cues support the skill that is being measured and reported. *Example: Feedback on operations being used while a student is completing a math task designed to assess the ability to select and use correct operations*

Source: Adapted from Jung, 2017c.

To begin, retention is not an evidence-based approach to improving student outcomes. In fact, the research is clear that retention yields *negative* outcomes for students (e.g., Hughes, Kwok, & Im, 2013). It's a somewhat different story if the student missed a significant portion of the year because of immigration, illness, or the like. In those cases, though, the student isn't exactly *repeating* the grade but rather starting where the curriculum left off. Even in these cases, retention may not be the answer.

On the surface, it seems logical that a student who is behind in 1st or 2nd grade would be able to "catch up" through repeating the grade. But we must remember that this student didn't miss every outcome of the current grade. The more sensible approach, then, is to identify the skills the student has not developed and provide targeted, research-based intervention (Jung, 2017d). Building those missing skills helps us head off what is an all-too-common situation: retained students who are initially on grade level but soon fall behind again, because the source of their difficulty was not addressed (Gleason, Kwok, & Hughes, 2007). Furthermore, retention tends to damage a student's self-esteem, and we know that a student's own expectations for outcomes predict success just as surely as a teacher's expectations do (Hattie, 2012). We must protect our students' belief in their ability to succeed.

Smarter Support for Students with IEPs

The IEP for every student who qualifies for special education services must include a general description of the services and support that the school will provide. But the IEP does not usually include the specific details of how everyone on the student's team will use those support strategies each day. The great ideas for specific strategies that come up at planning meetings are often not recorded. This means that members of the team who are not at the meeting might not deploy those strategies or, worse, that the strategies might be forgotten altogether.

The growth plan provides an important bridge between the IEP and what happens every day in the classroom. The detailed strategies are included in the growth plan and can be easily tweaked or revised based on how the student is performing. It's a setup that allows for smart, responsive support. Contrast this with the red tape associated with making a revision to an IEP document, which requires team meetings and signatures.

A Common Challenge: Disagreement About Best Strategies

Sometimes team members disagree about which strategies to use with a student. This disagreement can become heated and even result in power struggles within the team. At its worst, it can lead to team members using different strategies and not collaborating or communicating effectively.

To Prevent or Respond to the Challenge:

• Bear in mind that determining strategies comes down to the team's best guess of what will work. The evidence base should guide these decisions, along with what team members know about the individual student. Even so, it's still making an informed guess, and there are times when the team will guess wrong. Prepare the team for this possibility, and remind everyone that adjustments can and will be made when the data support change.

• Ensure team members have plenty of time to consider the strategies on the table and provide full feedback, but don't allow the discussion phase to carry on for hours. Leaders must be prepared to close the discussion, summarize the points, choose a strategy based on this input, and call for other team members to commit to trying that strategy.

• Don't expect everyone to agree that a certain strategy is best, but do lead the full team to commit to using it. Only through wholehearted implementation

continued

of the same strategy in the designated settings can we gather the data and determine if the strategy is, indeed, effective. This "disagree but commit" approach, borrowed from Intel and Amazon, allows the team to move forward with a plan in an efficient manner (Jung, 2017b).

CARMEN'S STORY

When Carmen's team turned to her goal of completing and turning in her homework independently, they talked about how support needed to "look for her." They knew Carmen wanted to complete and turn in her homework but struggled to do so. They used task analysis to map homework completion as a five-step process:

1. Take home the materials necessary to complete the homework.
2. Independently start the homework.
3. Finish the homework.
4. Take the homework to school.
5. Submit the homework to the teacher.

The team decided to use a checklist of the steps as a textual prompt in Carmen's agenda, and they paired this with backward chaining and prompt fading. Here is what they planned:

• Carmen will be given a direction for all five steps until she completes the process's final step herself.

• At this point, to implement backward chaining, the designated team members (Carmen's parents and subject-area teachers) will give Carmen a verbal reminder for the first four steps and no reminder for the last step (submitting the homework). These team members will monitor each step's completion.

- When Carmen submits on-time homework for one week with no reminder beyond step 4 (taking the homework to school), the team will issue reminders only through step 3 (finishing the homework). They will continue fading the prompts in this fashion.
- Regardless of the support Carmen needs to complete and turn in her homework, she will get full credit for doing so.

Summary

This chapter discussed the importance of working as interdisciplinary teams to select strategies to support a student's growth. Evidence-based strategies are those that research documents as effective. Teams should consider both academic and behavioral strategies and how they can use behavioral strategies to support academic skill development. Once teams select the strategies, they must map out exactly what implementation will look like, individualizing the strategies for the student and the classroom context.

Key Reminders:

- The task of selecting support strategies is not the responsibility of any one team member or discipline.
- Every student who has an IEP should have a growth plan and strategies, because the growth plan is what bridges the gap between the IEP and what happens every day in the classroom.
- By bringing common language on strategies to interdisciplinary teams, every team member can participate actively in crafting individualized strategies for the student.
- Behavioral strategies are useful for both behavior growth plans and academic ones. Students need support for their effort in persisting through difficult content and tasks.

- Strategies should be individualized to fit the unique qualities of the student and the specific settings in which the student participates.

With the full growth plan in place and implementation underway, all team members are ready to participate in collecting data on progress. The next chapter will explore how to use these data. It's the part of the process that gives teams vital direction for making focused and informed choices about instruction and intervention.

7

MEASURING PROGRESS AND USING DATA

Because there is a federal requirement for collecting progress data on IEP goals, it can feel like meeting this legal obligation is the primary purpose for the data collection teams do. But we must remember the reason behind the requirement, which exists to ensure we can analyze students' growth, examine the effectiveness of our interventions, and make the necessary adjustments. For this reason, it is important to measure the progress of every student, not just those with IEPs.

Data collection is the sixth and final step in the growth planning cycle, but in many ways, *using* that data is the first step in a new cycle, feeding into the next round of choosing critical skills, settings for intervention, goal attainment criteria, and growth-promoting strategies. Put simply, the data that teams collect inform instruction and intervention. This is data collection's most important function.

Who Collects Data and When?

Traditionally, it's been special educators who have been responsible for measuring progress on IEP goals and compiling all reports of progress—and for them, the final days before reports are due have typically been a stressful time. Much of this stress originates from having to bear the full responsibility of measuring progress and trying to report on goals that were not written to be measured in general education contexts.

Collecting progress data is an easier and much more meaningful task when teachers are able to do it within everyday classroom routines. This is especially true when measuring behavioral progress. It is not always possible to construct a situation to measure a student's self-advocacy skills, for example. But the general education teacher, who sees the student many hours per week, can easily report how much support the student needed to ask for assistance. Even with academic goals, it is often simpler to layer a measure of progress on an individualized goal over an existing classroom assessment than it is to create a new assessment situation, "trial," or "probe," as special educators have typically done in years past.

Here's a better model: Keep progress monitoring integrated with everyday classroom instruction and assessment. It's simpler logistically, of course, but having both general and special educators gather student data within the context of everyday observations and assessments is also the best way to ensure the data is meaningful. Whichever educator is naturally in the settings that teams chose for the growth plan should be taking data in that setting—using the agreed-to goal attainment scale and tracking mechanism. If everyone follows these guidelines, on the day that progress notes go home, the only major reporting task should be hitting "print" or "send."

High school teachers may be concerned about embedding data collection in the general education classroom. After all, each of these teachers may see more than 150 students every day. But with the task of data collection spread across multiple teachers, the schedule for data collection for each teacher can be relaxed. Consider a student whose growth plan includes four settings with four general education teachers. If each teacher records a progress measurement just once every two weeks, the student will have an average of two data points per week. If everyone on the team records data once a week or once every two weeks using the goal attainment scale, the data map will develop nicely into a picture that tells a comprehensive story of that student's progress.

The Value of Representing Data Visually

If data are to serve their primary function of informing instruction and intervention, everyone on the team must be able to understand the data. This can be best achieved if everyone collects data in the same systematic and simple way and presents it visually with charts or graphs (Schmid, 1954). Visuals help everyone understand the data, allowing all team members to participate more fully in data analysis, discussions of the student's process, and data-based decision making for the next steps in support. Charts and graphs are particularly useful when students' families have limited literacy skills or a different native language.

The Data Map

The procedures outlined in Chapters 3 and 4 for determining settings and using goal attainment scaling provide an easy path to capturing the data visually. The data map in Figure 7.1 includes four columns, each with a letter as a heading. These letters correspond with the letters for the established intervention settings. The number-color combinations on the data map align with the number-color combinations marking each level of performance on the goal attainment scale.

To record progress on this growth plan, the team member finds the column that corresponds with his or her setting and records the color-coded number that corresponds with the student's performance that day. For example, in

FIGURE 7.1 GROWTH PLAN DATA MAP

Data Map				+ ↗ ∧
Settings				
a language arts				
b social studies				
c science				
d learning support				

Date ▾	a	b	c	d
11/15/2016	4	4	-	4
11/09/2016	4	-	3.5	4
11/01/2016	-	4	-	4
10/27/2016	3.5	3.5	-	-
10/20/2016	-	4	3.5	3.5
10/11/2016	3.5	3	-	3
10/05/2016	3	-	3	3.5
09/28/2016	-	3.5	3	3
09/23/2016	-	3	-	3
09/19/2016	3	-	3	-
09/13/2016	2.5	3.5	-	3
09/07/2016	2.5	-	2.5	-
08/30/2016	-	-	2.5	2.5
05/11/2016	2.5	2	-	2
05/06/2016	2	-	-	2.5
04/26/2016	2	2	2	-
04/20/2016	-	2	1.5	2

Figure 7.1, if the "a" setting is language arts, and the "2.0" corresponds with one error per paragraph, we can see the student performed at that level in language arts on April 26 and May 6. As data are entered across settings for a few weeks

to months, a color-coded data map begins to appear. As we can see in Figure 7.1, this student's progress was relatively even across all settings.

As team members, families should have ongoing opportunities to review data and even collect it, if they desire. Not all families will be interested in recording progress data for their children, but having data from home and school can be incredibly enlightening! Contrasting patterns can spark important conversations about what everyone is doing in those different settings and what seems to work best. Examining data patterns and having these discussions can lead the team to design better strategies that work at both school and home. Consider behavioral challenges, for example, and how powerful this home-to-school collaboration would be.

In addition to the data map, teams may wish to represent data as a line graph. Although averaging data across time would make little sense, averaging data across *settings* for a day, as seen in Figure 7.2, produces a single data point for each day data were collected. The resulting line graph is familiar for many educators and families.

FIGURE 7.2 LINE GRAPH OF PROGRESS DATA

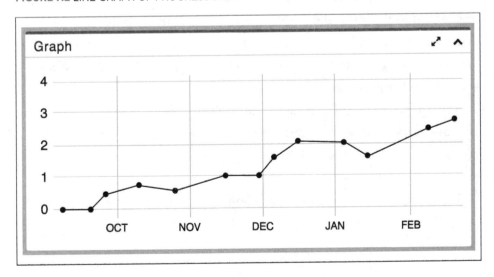

Online Data Collection

The simplest way for educators to generate data maps, graphs, and charts is through computer-assisted applications. Collecting data online makes it easier for many teachers to collaborate and contribute to the same data map. Online platforms also offer the ability to illustrate student progress by attaching samples of student work or videos of performance. Including samples of Carmen's writing a few times each year, for example, allows her team to clearly see the changes in progress. This side-by-side comparison of performance can be especially meaningful for students who have multiple disabilities and for whom progress may not always be obvious. For information on GoalWorks, the web-based platform featured in this book, visit GoalWorks.org.

Team Reflections and Progress Notes

In addition to assigning a score for a given performance, sometimes teams need to record narrative reflections and progress notes. Narratives are especially useful when there is additional information that the educator finds important that cannot be communicated by a single daily score. For example, a teacher may notice that Carmen performed much better today with her writing, and that teacher thinks the improved performance had something to do with Carmen's developing an online blog that she is excited about producing. This extra information can be helpful to the entire team as they continue to hone the strategies and support Carmen's growth.

The student should also engage in the reflective piece to the greatest extent possible. Students may have important insights or examples of their work from outside school that they would like to include. Every growth plan should have a place for these "aha" moments.

Figure 7.3 shows reflections that connect with Carmen's paragraph writing goal. Some web-based platforms, like GoalWorks, give teams the option of

FIGURE 7.3 REFLECTIONS

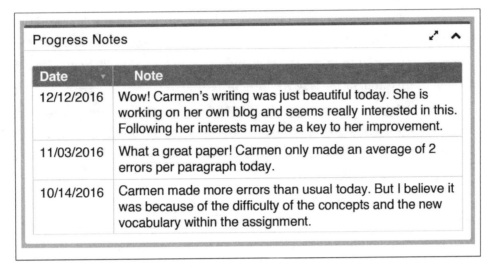

Progress Notes	⤢ ⌃

Date ▼	Note
12/12/2016	Wow! Carmen's writing was just beautiful today. She is working on her own blog and seems really interested in this. Following her interests may be a key to her improvement.
11/03/2016	What a great paper! Carmen only made an average of 2 errors per paragraph today.
10/14/2016	Carmen made more errors than usual today. But I believe it was because of the difficulty of the concepts and the new vocabulary within the assignment.

uploading samples of student performance or behavior in the form of a document, photo, or video file and attaching these to the progress note.

Analyzing Data

With a progress map emerging, teams have the chance to analyze the student's progress across settings and make decisions about continued support and intervention. Because data are captured and displayed consistently across students and teachers, everyone gains literacy with the data and can participate more efficiently in analysis and planning.

Rate of Progress

With a data map, members of the team can clearly see when intervention is working. The map shows exactly where a student is in relation to an annual goal at any point in time. Because there are nine increments of progress on the goal attainment scale and nine months in the academic year, teams should expect students to move up one increment per month.

Ideally, teams will see a clear progression from 0 to 4.0 over the course of the year. If this is the way the student's data map looks, then your team can celebrate a success! You chose the right strategy and implemented it well enough that it worked for this student the way you anticipated.

Unfortunately, even our best plans do not always work. The growth planning process is a problem-solving process in which team members come together to give their very best ideas on how to achieve student growth. But teams don't always get it right on the first go.

When the data map indicates a student is not progressing at the expected rate or the data are inconsistent, the team must ask why. Perhaps the strategies they chose were not the right ones or need to be revised in some way. The team might determine that they have not implemented the strategies long enough and need to allow more time for the chosen interventions to work.

Influences outside school may be affecting progress. If a student's family is struggling financially or interpersonally, or otherwise experiencing stress, this can affect a student's response to intervention. When a student is suffering from depression or anxiety, or is deficient in nutrition or sleep, progress may be more difficult. Talking to students so that these factors can be considered as part of the data analysis is critical. The team might decide to bring on new members, such as counselors, social workers, or psychologists, who can help make the interventions more effective.

Patterns of Data

In addition to examining rate of progress, teams can inspect the visual data for patterns. Because data are disaggregated by setting, teams will notice, for example, if a student is progressing differently in one setting. The data alone do not tell the team why this is happening, but the data should prompt discussion and problem-solving efforts. The team needs to ask questions about how the strategies are being implemented in each of the settings. What is happening in the setting in which progress is different?

For example, Carmen might be progressing very quickly on the components of her writing goal in her film studies class, but slower in the other settings. Is this because she is required to write shorter pieces in film class than she is in language arts and social students? Is it because film is Carmen's favorite class, and she is more engaged with this content? Maybe she's making faster progress in this class because the academic language was already familiar to her. Or perhaps her film studies teacher is implementing the strategies with more consistency. On the other hand, imagine if her performance lagged behind only in science. The team could ask questions such as, "Is this because the academic language in science is more difficult?" or, "Does she not enjoy science?" or, "Is the intervention not being delivered with fidelity in science?" Inquiry into what might be going on in this setting can help Carmen's team determine how to elevate her progress in the other settings.

A meeting to discuss the effectiveness of the plan should be triggered any time we see patterns of data that are inconsistent or too slow moving. Case managers can check student data each week or two for evidence of these patterns and convene teams for conversation and problem solving when progress isn't as expected. As with all aspects of the growth planning process, families and students should participate in these discussions to the greatest extent possible.

Including Students in Data Review

Whenever possible, students should be active in reviewing their own growth and contributing their own evidence. This process of checking in on growth on individualized goals is separate from the typical feedback students receive on individual tasks as a part of everyday classroom assessment. It threads through the curriculum and across times of day to provide a comprehensive view of a single skill. Most students, even younger ones, can understand the color-coded data map of their progress with an adult's guidance. Students may have great ideas to share with the team on why strategies are working well, or why they are not. They may also have ideas for new strategies to try.

This student engagement with progress data should happen on a regular basis as part of the implementation of the plan. Data collection, reflection, and revision of strategies should always feel like something we are doing *with* students, not *to* them. Teachers may schedule time or ask students to schedule time weekly, for example, for taking a look at their progress data and reflecting on their growth. This process may be independent for some students or guided by a mentor teacher for others.

A Common Challenge: Inconsistent Data Collection

It is important that all team members participate in data collection and do so regularly (not just before a formal report is due). But it's often the case that some are more diligent about collecting data than others. In some schools, this is a holdover from the days when students with learning differences were presumed to "belong" to special educators. In others, it's a casualty of workload or just simple oversight. Educators, being human and charged with managing a host of responsibilities, may let progress monitoring slip off the radar and forget to take data for one or many students.

Although there is room for some flexibility in the number of data points each team member contributes, without regular input from all settings, it becomes difficult to conduct a comprehensive analysis of student progress and make data-based decisions.

To Prevent and Respond to the Challenge:

- Work scrupulously to build a schoolwide culture in which "all students belong to all of us."

- Take steps to boost the progress-monitoring confidence of general educators who worry that special educators alone possess the necessary expertise to collect data on the growth of students with learning differences. One way to do this is to arrange for a special educator to gather data alongside the general educator until he or she is comfortable with data collection as a part of the daily routine.

- Formalize a policy by which all educators take data with a certain frequency for every student who has a growth plan associated with that educator's setting. For example, the school might decide that each person on the team of students receiving support within the general education classroom (Tier 2 support) must collect data at least twice per month. The requirement for students receiving intensive (Tier 3) support might be data collection at least once a week. Each school needs to determine a reasonable but appropriate frequency and make it policy.

- Automate reminders to collect data. Within GoalWorks, educators are automatically reminded to take data for each goal with which they are associated. Similar automation can be arranged via e-mail.

CARMEN'S STORY

In the preceding chapters, we've used Carmen's story to illustrate the steps of developing a growth plan. Figures 7.4, 7.5, and 7.6 show Carmen's completed growth plans with data.

You will notice that there are many blank spaces within Carmen's data maps. That is because not every teacher collected data on the same day. There may be days when data are recorded in only one setting, and this is fine. These spaces do not disrupt the team's ability to see and interpret Carmen's progress. There are ample data points, and together the points form a useful visual that will inform the team's

FIGURE 7.4 CARMEN'S GROWTH PLAN FOR CONVENTIONS OF WRITING

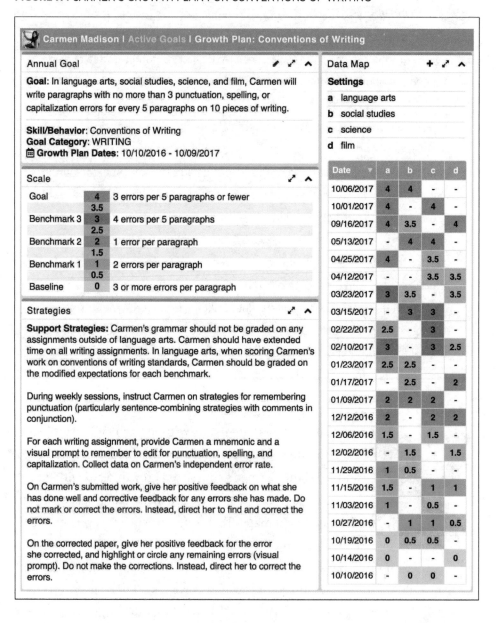

Carmen Madison I Active Goals I Growth Plan: Conventions of Writing

Annual Goal

Goal: In language arts, social studies, science, and film, Carmen will write paragraphs with no more than 3 punctuation, spelling, or capitalization errors for every 5 paragraphs on 10 pieces of writing.

Skill/Behavior: Conventions of Writing
Goal Category: WRITING
📅 **Growth Plan Dates:** 10/10/2016 - 10/09/2017

Scale

Goal	4	3 errors per 5 paragraphs or fewer
	3.5	
Benchmark 3	3	4 errors per 5 paragraphs
	2.5	
Benchmark 2	2	1 error per paragraph
	1.5	
Benchmark 1	1	2 errors per paragraph
	0.5	
Baseline	0	3 or more errors per paragraph

Strategies

Support Strategies: Carmen's grammar should not be graded on any assignments outside of language arts. Carmen should have extended time on all writing assignments. In language arts, when scoring Carmen's work on conventions of writing standards, Carmen should be graded on the modified expectations for each benchmark.

During weekly sessions, instruct Carmen on strategies for remembering punctuation (particularly sentence-combining strategies with comments in conjunction).

For each writing assignment, provide Carmen a mnemonic and a visual prompt to remember to edit for punctuation, spelling, and capitalization. Collect data on Carmen's independent error rate.

On Carmen's submitted work, give her positive feedback on what she has done well and corrective feedback for any errors she has made. Do not mark or correct the errors. Instead, direct her to find and correct the errors.

On the corrected paper, give her positive feedback for the error she corrected, and highlight or circle any remaining errors (visual prompt). Do not make the corrections. Instead, direct her to correct the errors.

Data Map

Settings
a language arts
b social studies
c science
d film

Date	a	b	c	d
10/06/2017	4	4	-	-
10/01/2017	4	-	4	-
09/16/2017	4	3.5	-	4
05/13/2017	-	4	4	-
04/25/2017	4	-	3.5	-
04/12/2017	-	-	3.5	3.5
03/23/2017	3	3.5	-	3.5
03/15/2017	-	3	3	-
02/22/2017	2.5	-	3	-
02/10/2017	3	-	3	2.5
01/23/2017	2.5	2.5	-	-
01/17/2017	-	2.5	-	2
01/09/2017	2	2	2	-
12/12/2016	2	-	2	2
12/06/2016	1.5	-	1.5	-
12/02/2016	-	1.5	-	1.5
11/29/2016	1	0.5	-	-
11/15/2016	1.5	-	1	1
11/03/2016	1	-	0.5	-
10/27/2016	-	1	1	0.5
10/19/2016	0	0.5	0.5	-
10/14/2016	0	-	-	0
10/10/2016	-	0	0	-

FIGURE 7.5 CARMEN'S GROWTH PLAN FOR EXPOSITORY WRITING

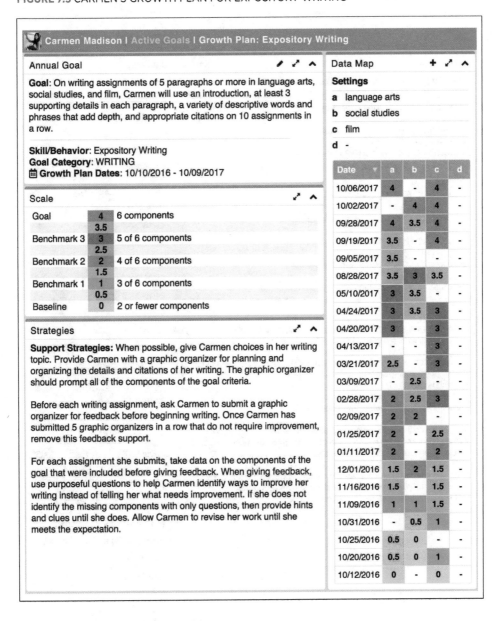

Carmen Madison I Active Goals I Growth Plan: Expository Writing

Annual Goal

Goal: On writing assignments of 5 paragraphs or more in language arts, social studies, and film, Carmen will use an introduction, at least 3 supporting details in each paragraph, a variety of descriptive words and phrases that add depth, and appropriate citations on 10 assignments in a row.

Skill/Behavior: Expository Writing
Goal Category: WRITING
Growth Plan Dates: 10/10/2016 - 10/09/2017

Scale

Goal	4	6 components
	3.5	
Benchmark 3	3	5 of 6 components
	2.5	
Benchmark 2	2	4 of 6 components
	1.5	
Benchmark 1	1	3 of 6 components
	0.5	
Baseline	0	2 or fewer components

Strategies

Support Strategies: When possible, give Carmen choices in her writing topic. Provide Carmen with a graphic organizer for planning and organizing the details and citations of her writing. The graphic organizer should prompt all of the components of the goal criteria.

Before each writing assignment, ask Carmen to submit a graphic organizer for feedback before beginning writing. Once Carmen has submitted 5 graphic organizers in a row that do not require improvement, remove this feedback support.

For each assignment she submits, take data on the components of the goal that were included before giving feedback. When giving feedback, use purposeful questions to help Carmen identify ways to improve her writing instead of telling her what needs improvement. If she does not identify the missing components with only questions, then provide hints and clues until she does. Allow Carmen to revise her work until she meets the expectation.

Data Map

Settings

a language arts
b social studies
c film
d -

Date	a	b	c	d
10/06/2017	4	-	4	-
10/02/2017	-	4	4	-
09/28/2017	4	3.5	4	-
09/19/2017	3.5	-	4	-
09/05/2017	3.5	-	-	-
08/28/2017	3.5	3	3.5	-
05/10/2017	3	3.5	-	-
04/24/2017	3	3.5	3	-
04/20/2017	3	-	3	-
04/13/2017	-	-	3	-
03/21/2017	2.5	-	3	-
03/09/2017	-	2.5	-	-
02/28/2017	2	2.5	3	-
02/09/2017	2	2	-	-
01/25/2017	2	-	2.5	-
01/11/2017	2	-	2	-
12/01/2016	1.5	2	1.5	-
11/16/2016	1.5	-	1.5	-
11/09/2016	1	1	1.5	-
10/31/2016	-	0.5	1	-
10/25/2016	0.5	0	-	-
10/20/2016	0.5	0	1	-
10/12/2016	0	-	0	-

FIGURE 7.6 CARMEN'S GROWTH PLAN FOR SUBMITTING HOMEWORK

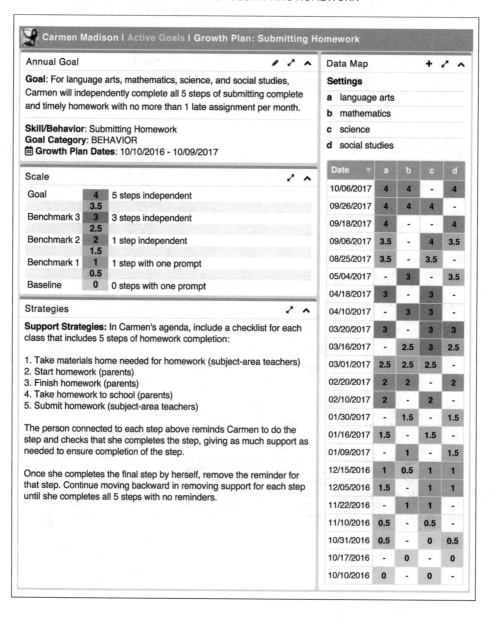

next steps. We can see from Carmen's data maps that she is progressing on her goals at a rate of one step on the goal attainment scale per month—the expected rate of progress. We can also see that her progress is fairly uniform across settings, indicating that the strategies are working well in each. It would stand to reason, then, that the team should continue implementing the current strategies until she has met the goal criteria.

Summary

Data collection, like growth plan development, is an interdisciplinary process in which every member of the team plays a role in monitoring student learning or behavior and recording information. The majority of this information should be recorded quantitatively—and in a way that allows for visual presentation. This facilitates data analysis and helps the team make important decisions about what is working, what is not, and where changes may be needed.

In addition to quantitative data, teams should record qualitative data when there is value in explaining more about the student's performance. Samples of student work and behavior documented in photographs and on video are important supplements that can enrich the support process. With these supplemental documents, teams have more substance to guide their conversations at meetings. And, with effective support strategies in place, they have concrete examples that facilitate celebration of successes!

Examining data across settings provides information on students' generalization of skills. The data do not always provide us with the answers to questions about why a student's skills are not generalizing to all settings, but they are the best means we have of ensuring our decisions are systematic and grounded in real and evolving needs. Keeping data disaggregated by setting is essential for making decisions that support transfer.

Key Reminders:

- The most important function of data is to inform instruction and intervention.
- If everyone takes data in the same systematic and simple way, and if those data are presented visually, everyone on the team can understand the data and make a better contribution to ongoing planning and support.
- Narrative progress notes are useful to convey important information that cannot be captured by one of the growth attainment scale's numeric scores.
- Teams should examine data for both rate of progress as well as patterns of progress. This review should lead to revisions to the plan when needed.
- Students who have growth plans should be active in reviewing their progress data and helping to revise strategies.

With the six growth planning steps covered, you should have a clear idea of what is involved and all there is to gain from this interdisciplinary approach to support and intervention. In the next chapter, we'll look at practical ways to implement it.

RECOMMENDATIONS
FOR GETTING STARTED

8

As this book has illustrated, when a clear process is in place, designing and using growth plans is not difficult. In fact, although the process is a deeper dive into individual skills, the goal attainment scale offers a simplified way for measuring, displaying, and reflecting upon progress. The initial task of revamping an existing schoolwide instruction and intervention approach to follow this interdisciplinary, family-centered one is a significant undertaking for schools. Leaders may be wondering how to begin.

Clearly, revising every IEP goal for every student who has one or creating multiple growth plans for all students who do not have an IEP is not a feasible task to take on all at once. However, schools are making progress in this direction, and they have found a number of ways to initiate systematic growth planning.

Six Approaches to Consider

The overall challenge for every school is to determine the right way to implement growth planning that is manageable but promotes steady progress. The decision may hinge on factors such as size of the school, the number of support staff, the number of students with the IEPs, the number of students who are underperforming but do not have disability diagnoses, and whether the school wishes to write growth plans for every student or only those who are behind grade level. These and many other factors can come into play as schools make decisions about implementation. Because many schools wish to begin the process with students who have IEPs, this population may be the most significant consideration at first. The eventual goal for all schools should be to move this initiative beyond the population of students with IEPs and, ideally, expand it to include all students.

Option 1: Begin with One Grade Level and Grow the Process Forward

In this approach, a high school, for example, may choose to implement the growth planning process with all 9th graders and then expand the effort to add one new grade each year.

The advantage of piloting the process with a single grade-level team is that their lessons learned can guide implementation with subsequent grade levels. The downside is that this method takes years to implement fully. Another difficulty arises when families have children in multiple grades. Although the population of families with multiple children who have IEPs is small, discussion with these parents is crucial to avoid confusion, and their ideas will be very valuable. If initiating this process with all students at a given grade level, a school will need to ensure that families know it is being phased in, beginning with the single grade.

Option 2: Begin with One Growth Plan per Student

In this approach, every student in the school can reap the benefits of having a growth plan within the first year of implementation.

The feasibility of the "start with one plan per student" approach depends on every educator in the school being trained in and understanding the process, which can be a challenge unto itself. If schools choose this approach, teams might create a growth plan for the skill that is the family and student's greatest priority. If even this step seems too big of a leap, schools could begin with one growth plan for every student who has an IEP. Expansion for students who have IEPs can happen as IEPs are due for review. For students who don't have an IEP, a second growth plan can be added at a scheduled time, perhaps midway through year 1 or at the beginning of year 2.

Option 3: Begin with Growth Plans for Existing IEP Goals

This is the approach I've used the most frequently with schools. Using this method, all goals (good, bad, and ugly) from existing IEPs are used as the basis for growth plans. Teams work to develop the best scales possible to go with these goals. Then, as IEPs are due for revision, the new process of starting with the growth plan is used to develop the new IEPs.

This is perhaps the quickest way to full implementation. It can be a disadvantage if everyone in the school has not received appropriate training in the process before implementation begins. Change is often more successful if the work on culture and rationale precedes the work on procedures.

Option 4: Develop Growth Plans as IEPs Are Due, Then Expand to Students Without IEPs

In this approach, the growth planning process is applied for each student who has an IEP when it is time to review his or her IEP. Full implementation for students with IEPs is achieved within one year. Other students can be added the following year.

The advantage to this approach is that it provides a more measured start, allowing teams to evaluate each student carefully and create excellent growth plans for that student. The challenge is that teams who are not pressed to write a lot of growth attainment scales early on may take longer to master the process. There is also less of a full commitment in the beginning, which could lead some staff members to drift away from the practice.

Option 5: Start with the Most Challenging Circumstances

Some teams may choose to use this process to tackle the most significant academic and behavioral challenges they are facing as a school. It's an approach based on prioritization of needs, similar to the growth planning process's focus on selecting the most critical skills, and it sets the stage for effective widespread implementation by familiarizing staff with the framework for team problem solving.

Students with IEPs may or may not be the initial focus. For example, if the school sees that students with IEPs are receiving adequate support under the existing model, but there are students in upper grades who don't have IEPs and are reading on an elementary level, the latter may be the higher priority. Schools can move on to subsequent priorities once the first phase of implementation is well under way.

Option 6: Begin with a Designated Type of Goal

With this approach, a school might target behavioral goals or academic goals or even one type of academic goal (e.g., writing goals) as a place to begin.

Many schools have existing initiatives in place that could parallel the move to the growth planning process. For example, a school that is working to implement restorative justice may wish to initiate this new way of planning IEPs for students who have behavioral challenges that aren't adequately met by this Tier 1 approach. For a school that is conducting a schoolwide writing intervention, a rollout focused on developing math-related growth plans for all students who need support in math might make the most sense.

The Challenge, the Work, and Why It Matters

Team development of systematic growth plans requires an understanding of research-based strategies, methods of measurement, and, most of all, intentional engagement in problem solving. This comprehensive, individualized planning results in data that the team can use and an organized plan that can transfer with a student to a new team or school, bringing cohesion to a student's experience from year to year.

Although this process requires a front-loading of staff time, once a growth plan is in place, very little effort is required to measure and report progress. By shifting the most significant efforts of intervention to the planning portion, all the support and measurement that follows is more meaningful—and much simpler. This investment into developing clear plans and systems of measurement is the key to meeting the needs of all our learners and moving every one of them from goals to growth.

APPENDIXES
STUDENT STORIES

APPENDIX A
Growth Planning for Carter

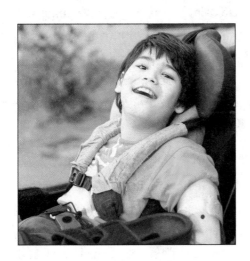

Carter is a 6th grade boy who qualifies for special education services because of cerebral palsy and a cognitive difference. He has a positive disposition most of the time and likes his time at school. The students in his general education classes enjoy his company and do a wonderful job including him in daily routines. Carter's best friend also receives special education services, and the boys have been in school together for the past four years. Carter spends two-thirds of his day in general education classrooms and one-third in a resource classroom. In addition to special instruction, Carter receives physical therapy, occupational therapy, and speech therapy—each once per week. With his wheelchair, Carter is able to get where he needs to go independently.

Carter has speech and can communicate with others. His speech can be difficult to understand for those who don't know him, and he does sometimes become frustrated when others don't understand him quickly. Carter is learning to read and currently is reading kindergarten-level text. He is developing the ability to write and can write his name somewhat legibly with trunk support, a secured paper, and a modified pencil. He can copy shapes and letters and can write some words independently. Carter can count objects to 10 and can sort objects by one characteristic. He is ready to work on adding with objects.

The Team Meeting

The people who attended Carter's annual IEP review included Carter; both of his parents; one 6th grade general education teacher; and his special education teacher, physical therapist, speech therapist, and occupational therapist. Carter's special education teacher, Kim, is also Carter's service coordinator, and she led the meeting.

Kim greeted everyone and began by describing how she had enjoyed working with Carter over the past year and was thrilled to see his progress in learning to read text. "This time last year, he was only able to name a few letters, and now he is reading words!" she said. "It's been so exciting to watch." Kim asked Carter's parents to bring everyone up to speed on Carter's interests and activities over the summer.

Carter's mom, Stacy, began. "Carter learned to swim this summer," she said. Carter perked up and smiled, clearly proud of his accomplishment. "He enjoyed the water and wanted so much to be able to pass the swimming test at the YMCA so he could use all of the pools," Stacy continued. "He worked so hard on the requirements. Midway through the summer, he passed the test. Toward the end of the summer, he was even using the diving board!"

Carter's dad, Gerald, then talked about how he and Carter had enjoyed watching movies together over the summer. "Carter has become quite the *Star Wars* fan," Gerald said. Kim smiled and joked, "That's not exactly a coincidence, given your love for *Star Wars*, Gerald!"

Target Area: Reading Decoding

Gerald commented that he was pleased to see Carter use his new reading skills this summer: "Carter's world has opened up now that he can read signs and other words he sees when we are out."

Carter's 6th grade teacher, Allison, offered a suggestion: "I could really work with the *Star Wars* theme in finding reading materials to engage Carter across all of his classes." Allison turned to Carter and asked, "Carter, would you enjoy reading about space and reading action stories this year?" Carter smiled and gave an enthusiastic "Uh-huh!"

Service coordinator Kim asked Carter's parents if he had continued using the iPad apps they'd selected last spring to support his reading. Stacy confirmed they had. "We stuck to a reading schedule of three times per week for the most part all summer," she said, "and we found several other apps that he enjoyed, too." Kim said she believed Carter could be reading on a mid–1st grade level within a year. "That would be so wonderful to see," Stacy said.

Target Area: Addition

Allison, the classroom teacher, then described the 6th grade expectations in mathematics, using the framework of domains within the Common Core State Standards.

Kim pointed out that many standards within the domains build on the ability to group like items and add single digits to 10. The team agreed that Carter had made significant progress with counting and sorting objects and was ready to continue his work on adding. They decided to target adding numbers up to 10, using objects for support. Allison suggested, "It would be easy to use items from the *Star Wars* universe or other space-related objects and pictures when we're working on this adding skill."

Target Area: Speech Articulation

Carter's speech therapist, Kelly, then described Carter's progress with speech and language. Carter, like most people with cerebral palsy, has hypertonia, or high muscle tone. Hypertonia makes articulation difficult for Carter, so this skill has been a target. Stacy noted, "We have seen improvement, and I can almost always understand what he's saying. But so many people still have a hard time understanding Carter, and this frustrates him." Gerald agreed, saying, "Carter has more trouble when he is tired—both with speech as well as handling the frustration."

Kelly agreed that articulation should still be a priority and suggested a communication device. Stacy and Gerald looked at each other. They had declined the use of a communication device in the past, they explained, because they were concerned it might prevent Carter from learning to talk. Having learned more about communication devices, and having come to terms with the long-term nature of Carter's need for support with speech, they now agreed it was something Carter ought to try. Gerald asked, "Can speech still be something we work on, even after we get him a communication device?" The team agreed that helping Carter to communicate in multiple ways was the objective—and these efforts would logically include articulation of speech, even if Carter began using an assistive device. They decided to revisit setting a speech support goal for Carter when a communication device had been ordered and received.

Target Area: Fine Motor Skills

Next, Carter's team discussed the fine motor skills of writing and drawing. Carter had made wonderful progress with both over the past year. His occupational therapist, Mishka, described how he had learned to write some words and copy shapes and letters using the adapted pencil.

Mishka asked, "How is using the adapted pencils at home going?" Stacy responded, "I wasn't seeing a lot of progress with his drawing or writing, but then I realized the problem was the time of day I was suggesting he write or draw. Carter is usually tired at the end of the school day. After a whole day at school, it's physically more difficult for him to sit without support and use his fine motor skills. So I started suggesting Carter draw and write in the morning on the weekends. It goes really well!"

Gerald shifted the conversation slightly. "When Carter gets home from school, he just needs to decompress and relax like the rest of us," he said. "Stacy and I have been down the road of trying to serve as his therapists, and that's not what we want. That doesn't work for any of us."

Kim suggested that the team look at ways to limit homework for Carter to accommodate his need for more downtime in the evenings. Classroom teacher Allison agreed and noted that the 6th grade instructional team could easily make this accommodation.

After a bit more discussion, the team decided that Carter should continue with a writing-focused goal and that they would like to see him able to write all letters legibly. "If Carter could build stamina for writing longer than five minutes at a time, I'm confident his skills in writing will improve," Kim said. Everyone nodded in agreement, and Mishka added, "That would be a great goal—to build his persistence in writing to 15–20 minutes."

Priorities

Through these conversations, the team identified the critical skills they wanted Carter to focus on and set the annual goals for Carter's IEP (see Figure A.1). All of Carter's goals could be measured in both his general education classroom and learning support classroom.

FIGURE A.1 CRITICAL SKILLS AND ANNUAL GOALS FOR CARTER

Critical Skills	Annual Goals
Reading 1st grade texts with understanding	In language arts, social studies, and learning support class, Carter will read 1st grade text and accurately respond to questions about major details with no more than one error per five questions on 15 passages.
Adding numbers up to 10, using objects	In mathematics, science, art, and learning support class, Carter will correctly add all numbers through 10 with no more than one error per 10 problems on five assessments.
Persisting with writing tasks for at least 20 minutes without frustration or discomfort	During language arts, social studies, learning support, and art, Carter will persist in writing tasks using an adapted pencil for at least 20 minutes without discomfort or frustration on four of five days.

Strategies

Next, Carter's team turned to the task of determining strategies for each of his goals. Across the board, they planned to incorporate his new interest in space and *Star Wars* to build his engagement.

For Carter's reading goal, Kim suggested the strategy of dialogic reading be used to build Carter's comprehension and vocabulary with increasingly complex text. Kim explained to his parents that she could video herself using dialogic reading and show them how they could do it at home.

For mathematics, Kim suggested the use of manipulatives and photos to build Carter's number sense. Classroom teacher Allison added, "I have ideas of how we can use objects and how to make games using the space and *Star Wars* theme."

For writing and drawing, Mishka suggested the continued use of the adapted pencil. Carter's physical therapist, Josh, had a question: "Carter has grown a lot over the summer, hasn't he?" "More than an inch," Stacy responded. Josh suggested taking a close look at Carter's chair and tray to see if it needed to be adjusted to better support writing and drawing. Mishka also had ideas for using a timer and soft music during writing time to build Carter's stamina.

Carter's Growth Plans

The team developed three growth plans for Carter, shown in Figures A.2, A.3, and A.4.

Team Reflection and Revision

After implementing each of Carter's growth plans and collecting and entering data into an online application, the team was able to see a clear pattern of his progress.

Interestingly, for each of Carter's goals, he mastered the benchmark measured within the learning support class most quickly, and those data showed he was clearly able to generalize his new skills to the general education classroom, too. Because his progress was monitored in every classroom, the team could see that the intervention was working—and working to help

FIGURE A.2 CARTER'S GROWTH PLAN FOR DECODING

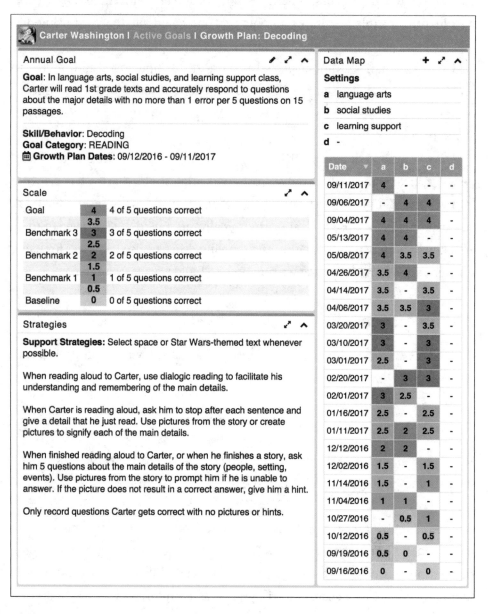

Carter Washington | Active Goals | Growth Plan: Decoding

Annual Goal

Goal: In language arts, social studies, and learning support class, Carter will read 1st grade texts and accurately respond to questions about the major details with no more than 1 error per 5 questions on 15 passages.

Skill/Behavior: Decoding
Goal Category: READING
📅 **Growth Plan Dates:** 09/12/2016 - 09/11/2017

Scale

Goal	**4**	4 of 5 questions correct
	3.5	
Benchmark 3	**3**	3 of 5 questions correct
	2.5	
Benchmark 2	**2**	2 of 5 questions correct
	1.5	
Benchmark 1	**1**	1 of 5 questions correct
	0.5	
Baseline	**0**	0 of 5 questions correct

Strategies

Support Strategies: Select space or Star Wars-themed text whenever possible.

When reading aloud to Carter, use dialogic reading to facilitate his understanding and remembering of the main details.

When Carter is reading aloud, ask him to stop after each sentence and give a detail that he just read. Use pictures from the story or create pictures to signify each of the main details.

When finished reading aloud to Carter, or when he finishes a story, ask him 5 questions about the main details of the story (people, setting, events). Use pictures from the story to prompt him if he is unable to answer. If the picture does not result in a correct answer, give him a hint.

Only record questions Carter gets correct with no pictures or hints.

Data Map

Settings
a language arts
b social studies
c learning support
d -

Date	a	b	c	d
09/11/2017	4	-	-	-
09/06/2017	-	4	4	-
09/04/2017	4	4	4	-
05/13/2017	4	4	-	-
05/08/2017	4	3.5	3.5	-
04/26/2017	3.5	4	-	-
04/14/2017	3.5	-	3.5	-
04/06/2017	3.5	3.5	3	-
03/20/2017	3	-	3.5	-
03/10/2017	3	-	3	-
03/01/2017	2.5	-	3	-
02/20/2017	-	3	3	-
02/01/2017	3	2.5	-	-
01/16/2017	2.5	-	2.5	-
01/11/2017	2.5	2	2.5	-
12/12/2016	2	2	-	-
12/02/2016	1.5	-	1.5	-
11/14/2016	1.5	-	1	-
11/04/2016	1	1	-	-
10/27/2016	-	0.5	1	-
10/12/2016	0.5	-	0.5	-
09/19/2016	0.5	0	-	-
09/16/2016	0	-	0	-

FIGURE A.3 CARTER'S GROWTH PLAN FOR ADDITION

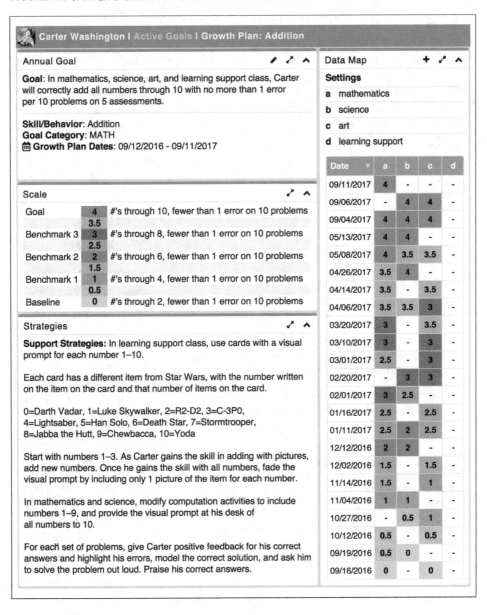

Carter Washington I Active Goals I Growth Plan: Addition

Annual Goal

Goal: In mathematics, science, art, and learning support class, Carter will correctly add all numbers through 10 with no more than 1 error per 10 problems on 5 assessments.

Skill/Behavior: Addition
Goal Category: MATH
Growth Plan Dates: 09/12/2016 - 09/11/2017

Scale

Goal	**4**	#'s through 10, fewer than 1 error on 10 problems
	3.5	
Benchmark 3	**3**	#'s through 8, fewer than 1 error on 10 problems
	2.5	
Benchmark 2	**2**	#'s through 6, fewer than 1 error on 10 problems
	1.5	
Benchmark 1	**1**	#'s through 4, fewer than 1 error on 10 problems
	0.5	
Baseline	**0**	#'s through 2, fewer than 1 error on 10 problems

Strategies

Support Strategies: In learning support class, use cards with a visual prompt for each number 1–10.

Each card has a different item from Star Wars, with the number written on the item on the card and that number of items on the card.

0=Darth Vadar, 1=Luke Skywalker, 2=R2-D2, 3=C-3PO, 4=Lightsaber, 5=Han Solo, 6=Death Star, 7=Stormtrooper, 8=Jabba the Hutt, 9=Chewbacca, 10=Yoda

Start with numbers 1–3. As Carter gains the skill in adding with pictures, add new numbers. Once he gains the skill with all numbers, fade the visual prompt by including only 1 picture of the item for each number.

In mathematics and science, modify computation activities to include numbers 1–9, and provide the visual prompt at his desk of all numbers to 10.

For each set of problems, give Carter positive feedback for his correct answers and highlight his errors, model the correct solution, and ask him to solve the problem out loud. Praise his correct answers.

Data Map

Settings
a mathematics
b science
c art
d learning support

Date	a	b	c	d
09/11/2017	4	-	-	-
09/06/2017	-	4	4	-
09/04/2017	4	4	4	-
05/13/2017	4	4	-	-
05/08/2017	4	3.5	3.5	-
04/26/2017	3.5	4	-	-
04/14/2017	3.5	-	3.5	-
04/06/2017	3.5	3.5	3	-
03/20/2017	3	-	3.5	-
03/10/2017	3	-	3	-
03/01/2017	2.5	-	3	-
02/20/2017	-	3	3	-
02/01/2017	3	2.5	-	-
01/16/2017	2.5	-	2.5	-
01/11/2017	2.5	2	2.5	-
12/12/2016	2	2	-	-
12/02/2016	1.5	-	1.5	-
11/14/2016	1.5	-	1	-
11/04/2016	1	1	-	-
10/27/2016	-	0.5	1	-
10/12/2016	0.5	-	0.5	-
09/19/2016	0.5	0	-	-
09/16/2016	0	-	0	-

FIGURE A.4 CARTER'S GROWTH PLAN FOR WRITING PERSISTENCE

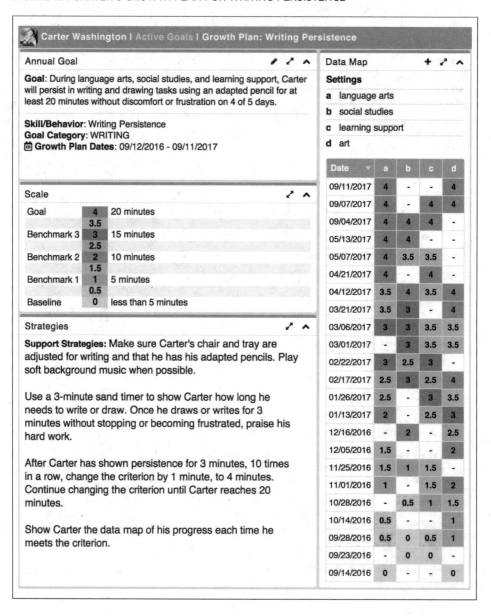

Carter Washington I Active Goals I Growth Plan: Writing Persistence

Annual Goal

Goal: During language arts, social studies, and learning support, Carter will persist in writing and drawing tasks using an adapted pencil for at least 20 minutes without discomfort or frustration on 4 of 5 days.

Skill/Behavior: Writing Persistence
Goal Category: WRITING
Growth Plan Dates: 09/12/2016 - 09/11/2017

Scale

Goal	**4**	20 minutes
	3.5	
Benchmark 3	**3**	15 minutes
	2.5	
Benchmark 2	**2**	10 minutes
	1.5	
Benchmark 1	**1**	5 minutes
	0.5	
Baseline	**0**	less than 5 minutes

Strategies

Support Strategies: Make sure Carter's chair and tray are adjusted for writing and that he has his adapted pencils. Play soft background music when possible.

Use a 3-minute sand timer to show Carter how long he needs to write or draw. Once he draws or writes for 3 minutes without stopping or becoming frustrated, praise his hard work.

After Carter has shown persistence for 3 minutes, 10 times in a row, change the criterion by 1 minute, to 4 minutes. Continue changing the criterion until Carter reaches 20 minutes.

Show Carter the data map of his progress each time he meets the criterion.

Data Map

Settings

a language arts
b social studies
c learning support
d art

Date	a	b	c	d
09/11/2017	4	-	-	4
09/07/2017	4	-	4	4
09/04/2017	4	4	4	-
05/13/2017	4	4	-	-
05/07/2017	4	3.5	3.5	-
04/21/2017	4	-	4	-
04/12/2017	3.5	4	3.5	4
03/21/2017	3.5	3	-	4
03/06/2017	3	3	3.5	3.5
03/01/2017	-	3	3.5	3.5
02/22/2017	3	2.5	3	-
02/17/2017	2.5	3	2.5	4
01/26/2017	2.5	-	3	3.5
01/13/2017	2	-	2.5	3
12/16/2016	-	2	-	2.5
12/05/2016	1.5	-	-	2
11/25/2016	1.5	1	1.5	-
11/01/2016	1	-	1.5	2
10/28/2016	-	0.5	1	1.5
10/14/2016	0.5	-	-	1
09/28/2016	0.5	0	0.5	1
09/23/2016	-	0	0	-
09/14/2016	0	-	-	0

Carter not only collect new skills but also use those skills successfully in inclusive settings. Because this was Carter's pattern of progress, the team knew to keep implementing the plan as originally designed. Had he not made progress in one of the settings, for example, the team would've convened to discuss the possible contributing factors. Next, they would select the best possible solution and implement it. After making an adjustment, the team should meet again soon after the next data points are added to review the effectiveness of the change.

Questions for Reflection

Think of a student in your school who has a similar profile to Carter. What are some of the ways the planning process for this student compares and contrasts to the planning process for Carter? Specifically, consider the following:

1. How were related service providers included in the plan development? Were there separate "PT goals" and "special education goals" as opposed to Carter's interdisciplinary process?

2. Did the parents express a need to "just be parents," as Carter's did? Have you heard this need expressed by other parents of students with multiple disabilities?

3. Are goals for students with multiple disabilities typically written in a way that makes growth clear? Or do goals look essentially the same from year to year?

APPENDIX B
Growth Planning for Maggie

Maggie is a 9th grade student who qualifies for special education services because of a diagnosis of autism spectrum disorder.

Maggie has been attending an American international school in Bogotá, Colombia, for the past three years. Her mother was recently offered a promotion that would have required a move to a different country, but Maggie has been doing so well at Colegio Bogotá that her parents, Laura and Brian, decided the best choice was to stay in Bogotá until she graduates. Maggie attends co-taught general education classes all day, with the exception of one hour of learning support, which is set aside for targeted intervention and additional time to work on assignments. Maggie is now working close to grade level in all subject areas except for the speaking standards in language arts.

Maggie's teachers have also been working with her to become more independent in the routines of school. In particular, she receives support in the areas of managing time and materials, regulating her emotions, and initiating and maintaining conversation with her classmates.

The Team Meeting

Maggie's IEP meeting was due in December and held in the evening, when parents Laura and Brian were off from work. Others who attended included Maggie's language arts/homeroom teacher, her learning support teacher, the special education coordinator for the campus, and Maggie herself.

Everyone met in the learning support classroom. Laura and Brian have two younger children who attend the school, too, and they are very involved with many school activities. Because of this, and because of the many meetings that have been held over the years to plan for Maggie, everyone at the meeting knew each other well.

The special education coordinator, Chad, called the meeting to order.: "Thanks, everyone, for making time for our meeting today. Let's get started."

As everyone took a seat, Chad asked Maggie and her parents how they thought the year was going so far.

Maggie's dad, Brian, was enthusiastic as he described how pleased he was with Maggie's progress in school: "She's getting closer and closer to being on grade level each year. It's just remarkable what's she's accomplished." Maggie had been late to develop verbal language and lagged behind in many subjects all through elementary school. She still struggles some with verbal language, especially when frustrated, but her progress had really taken off since beginning at Colegio Bogotá. Maggie's mom, Laura, agreed, looking at Maggie and then back to the team, saying, "You all, I am just so grateful to the whole learning support team and all of her teachers at Colegio Bogotá. I don't know what we would have done without you." Maggie's special education teacher, Natalie, complimented Maggie on her hard work. "Maggie, you have really gotten into your schoolwork this year," she said. "We are so proud of you for working so hard and sticking with work that is hard." Maggie looked down and smiled.

Target Area: Handling Transitions

Natalie started by describing Maggie's persistence when tasks are difficult. She commented that sometimes Maggie's persistence was so good, in fact, that she had difficulty transitioning to a new activity. Laura nodded in agreement, saying, "At home it's still hard to get Maggie to stop what she is doing when it's time to leave the house or have a meal, especially if it's an art project she's gotten really into."

Maggie's language arts teacher, Dori, agreed, describing Maggie's difficulty putting aside writing assignments when it was time for a class change. Dori explained that when Maggie is involved in a writing assignment and it is time to change classes, she continues to write. Everyone agreed that it is wonderful to see Maggie so involved in her writing assignments.

Dori elaborated, "When I walk to Maggie and tell her directly that it's time to go and start helping her to put her materials away, she often puts her face in her hands and pretends to cry. When this happens, she usually needs support to walk to her next class, and she continues the crying behavior until she's in the next classroom. She doesn't use any words at all when we are walking."

Natalie noted that a variation of this behavior was happening in many of Maggie's classes. The team agreed they would like to see Maggie become more independent by following the prompt to transition given to the whole class rather than needing individual help or directions.

Target Area: Regulating Emotion

Chad, the special education coordinator, added that transitions weren't the only time that Maggie gets upset and is unable to find words. "When she does get upset about something, rather than pretending to cry, I'd like to see her use words or some other way to express her emotion that is socially appropriate," he said. Maggie's mom, Laura, agreed: "Of course, I'd like to see Maggie go with the flow when it is time to change activities, but if she isn't happy about something, it would be great to see her show that with words or facial expressions instead of this crying behavior. She does it sometimes when we are out, and it brings a lot of attention to her that she doesn't like."

Target Area: Communicating and Interacting Socially

Classroom teacher Dori said she was happy to see the progress Maggie had made in joining her friends' conversations and activities. Laura cut in to express some concern, saying, "I know she is doing much better at school talking to others, but I can't help noticing that she is never invited to do anything with any of her classmates after school. To me, those kinds of invitations are an indication of whether she is *really* included, and she isn't." Everyone nodded in agreement.

Brian added, "It would be so wonderful to see her really belong to a group of friends the way our younger children do."

The team talked at length about long-term goals for Maggie to establish and maintain friendships in adulthood. In the end, the team decided that if Maggie's social conversation skills improved, she would more likely be included socially.

Maggie's speech therapist, Julie, had a suggestion: "Last year we spent time really helping Maggie to join in conversation with her friends during classes," she said. "What we *haven't* done is put a lot of effort into carrying that over to the nonacademic time like lunch and hanging out before and after school."

Natalie proposed that they observe Maggie during these times of the day to build a set of phrases and conversations that could help Maggie interact with her friends during social times. Her parents agreed that they wanted her to have more "social language" that could help her outside classes. Laura pointed out, "She gets to school 20 minutes early every day because of my work schedule, so there's plenty of before-school time for us to work with. She usually doesn't have to wait on us after school, but we could adjust our pick-up time and change that to provide more time for socialization then."

Priorities

Based on these conversations, the team listed the critical skills as priorities for Maggie and developed a set of annual goals for her IEP (see Figure B.1). Maggie's team discussed each of the main priorities and how they would like Maggie's skills in these areas to look at the end of a year.

Strategies

Maggie's special education teacher led the discussion of strategies. In thinking about the transition goal, Natalie suggested starting by using an auditory prompt

FIGURE B.1 CRITICAL SKILLS AND ANNUAL GOALS FOR MAGGIE

Critical Skills	Annual Goals
Transitioning between activities	When it is time to transition from language arts, science, art, and math, Maggie will put her work away and walk to the next class with only the direction given to the large group.
Regulating emotion	During classes, transitions, and at home, Maggie will independently use calm words when she is frustrated without pretending to cry more than once per week.
Initiating conversations with friends	Before school, during lunch, or after school, Maggie will initiate a conversation and remain engaged in it for at least 10 minutes at least 5 times per week.

to fade the need for an adult to be physically present to give individual directions and help Maggie put away her materials at the end of each class session. Classroom teacher Dori suggested, "Why don't we use the same sound for all transitions—the ones that go well *and* the ones that don't? I have a xylophone-style chime that I've used before. I think that might even help several other students be better prepared for a transition." Chad nodded and added, "We can get the chime for each of her teachers to use."

To support Maggie's growth on the communicating-when-frustrated goal, Natalie proposed using the social story strategy to help Maggie get into a routine of using new ways to communicate what she is thinking. "We might even start with a social story about transitioning from classes," she added, before turning to Laura and Brian and explaining, "A social story is one we create that lets us 'rewrite the script' Maggie is currently using. We can create one and then give a copy to you to use at home, too. I'd love to add other scripts to help address communication needs you might be seeing at home."

In order to support Maggie's initiation of conversation with friends during social times, the team agreed the first step was to plan opportunities for conversation. "We also need to support her with prompts at first, but it would be better to have students work with her than teachers," Natalie commented. Dori added, "I could choose several girls from the class to help us with this goal." The team then discussed how Maggie's peers could be enlisted to support this social interaction goal.

Maggie's Growth Plans

The three growth plans developed for Maggie are shown in Figures B.2, B.3, and B.4.

Team Reflection and Revision

With behavioral support plans like the ones put into place for Maggie's transition, teams really are customizing strategies in a way that is informed by evidence-based practices, but until we start to measure progress, we aren't sure if these are going to work. Highly individualized plans for supporting behavior rely on a solid functional behavior assessment that clarifies why the student is using certain behaviors.

Examining Maggie's data map, we see that the plan did, indeed, work. If she had not begun to make progress on the transition goal, the team might have returned to her functional behavioral assessment to see if there was anything they had missed—if they could have been wrong about the function of her behavior. Note that if they had decided to change strategies, they would have needed to start a new graph to ensure that data would be clearly connected

FIGURE B.2 MAGGIE'S GROWTH PLAN FOR TRANSITIONS

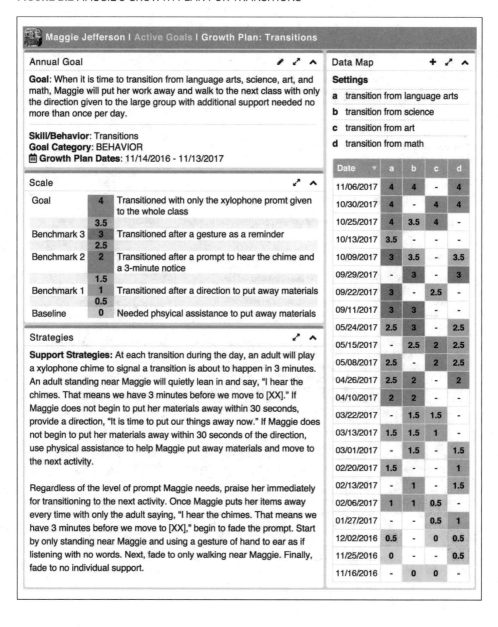

Maggie Jefferson I Active Goals I Growth Plan: Transitions

Annual Goal

Goal: When it is time to transition from language arts, science, art, and math, Maggie will put her work away and walk to the next class with only the direction given to the large group with additional support needed no more than once per day.

Skill/Behavior: Transitions
Goal Category: BEHAVIOR
📅 **Growth Plan Dates**: 11/14/2016 - 11/13/2017

Scale

Goal	4	Transitioned with only the xylophone promt given to the whole class
	3.5	
Benchmark 3	3	Transitioned after a gesture as a reminder
	2.5	
Benchmark 2	2	Transitioned after a prompt to hear the chime and a 3-minute notice
	1.5	
Benchmark 1	1	Transitioned after a direction to put away materials
	0.5	
Baseline	0	Needed phsyical assistance to put away materials

Strategies

Support Strategies: At each transition during the day, an adult will play a xylophone chime to signal a transition is about to happen in 3 minutes. An adult standing near Maggie will quietly lean in and say, "I hear the chimes. That means we have 3 minutes before we move to [XX]." If Maggie does not begin to put her materials away within 30 seconds, provide a direction, "It is time to put our things away now." If Maggie does not begin to put her materials away within 30 seconds of the direction, use physical assistance to help Maggie put away materials and move to the next activity.

Regardless of the level of prompt Maggie needs, praise her immediately for transitioning to the next activity. Once Maggie puts her items away every time with only the adult saying, "I hear the chimes. That means we have 3 minutes before we move to [XX]," begin to fade the prompt. Start by only standing near Maggie and using a gesture of hand to ear as if listening with no words. Next, fade to only walking near Maggie. Finally, fade to no individual support.

Data Map

Settings
- a transition from language arts
- b transition from science
- c transition from art
- d transition from math

Date	a	b	c	d
11/06/2017	4	4	-	4
10/30/2017	4	-	4	4
10/25/2017	4	3.5	4	-
10/13/2017	3.5	-	-	-
10/09/2017	3	3.5	-	3.5
09/29/2017	-	3	-	3
09/22/2017	3	-	2.5	-
09/11/2017	3	3	-	-
05/24/2017	2.5	3	-	2.5
05/15/2017	-	2.5	2	2.5
05/08/2017	2.5	-	2	2.5
04/26/2017	2.5	2	-	2
04/10/2017	2	2	-	-
03/22/2017	-	1.5	1.5	-
03/13/2017	1.5	1.5	1	-
03/01/2017	-	1.5	-	1.5
02/20/2017	1.5	-	-	1
02/13/2017	-	1	-	1.5
02/06/2017	1	1	0.5	-
01/27/2017	-	-	0.5	1
12/02/2016	0.5	-	0	0.5
11/25/2016	0	-	-	0.5
11/16/2016	-	0	0	-

FIGURE B.3 MAGGIE'S GROWTH PLAN FOR REGULATING EMOTION

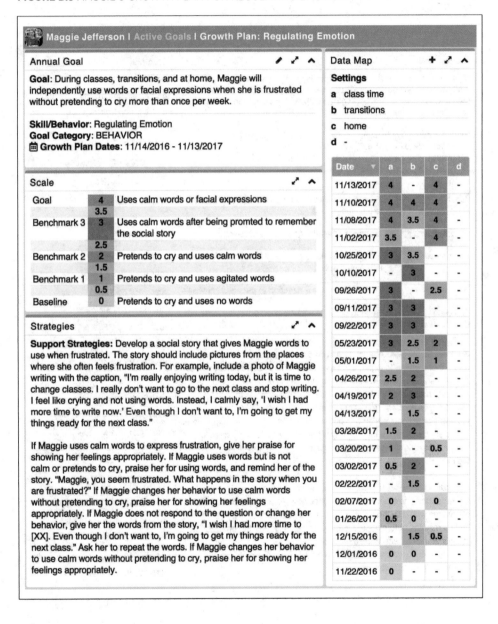

Maggie Jefferson | Active Goals | Growth Plan: Regulating Emotion

Annual Goal

Goal: During classes, transitions, and at home, Maggie will independently use words or facial expressions when she is frustrated without pretending to cry more than once per week.

Skill/Behavior: Regulating Emotion
Goal Category: BEHAVIOR
📅 **Growth Plan Dates**: 11/14/2016 - 11/13/2017

Scale

Goal	4	Uses calm words or facial expressions
	3.5	
Benchmark 3	3	Uses calm words after being promted to remember the social story
	2.5	
Benchmark 2	2	Pretends to cry and uses calm words
	1.5	
Benchmark 1	1	Pretends to cry and uses agitated words
	0.5	
Baseline	0	Pretends to cry and uses no words

Strategies

Support Strategies: Develop a social story that gives Maggie words to use when frustrated. The story should include pictures from the places where she often feels frustration. For example, include a photo of Maggie writing with the caption, "I'm really enjoying writing today, but it is time to change classes. I really don't want to go to the next class and stop writing. I feel like crying and not using words. Instead, I calmly say, 'I wish I had more time to write now.' Even though I don't want to, I'm going to get my things ready for the next class."

If Maggie uses calm words to express frustration, give her praise for showing her feelings appropriately. If Maggie uses words but is not calm or pretends to cry, praise her for using words, and remind her of the story. "Maggie, you seem frustrated. What happens in the story when you are frustrated?" If Maggie changes her behavior to use calm words without pretending to cry, praise her for showing her feelings appropriately. If Maggie does not respond to the question or change her behavior, give her the words from the story, "I wish I had more time to [XX]. Even though I don't want to, I'm going to get my things ready for the next class." Ask her to repeat the words. If Maggie changes her behavior to use calm words without pretending to cry, praise her for showing her feelings appropriately.

Data Map

Settings
a class time
b transitions
c home
d -

Date	a	b	c	d
11/13/2017	4	-	4	-
11/10/2017	4	4	4	-
11/08/2017	4	3.5	4	-
11/02/2017	3.5	-	4	-
10/25/2017	3	3.5	-	-
10/10/2017	-	3	-	-
09/26/2017	3	-	2.5	-
09/11/2017	3	3	-	-
09/22/2017	3	3	-	-
05/23/2017	3	2.5	2	-
05/01/2017	-	1.5	1	-
04/26/2017	2.5	2	-	-
04/19/2017	2	3	-	-
04/13/2017	-	1.5	-	-
03/28/2017	1.5	2	-	-
03/20/2017	1	-	0.5	-
03/02/2017	0.5	2	-	-
02/22/2017	-	1.5	-	-
02/07/2017	0	-	0	-
01/26/2017	0.5	0	-	-
12/15/2016	-	1.5	0.5	-
12/01/2016	0	0	-	-
11/22/2016	0	-	-	-

FIGURE B.4 MAGGIE'S GROWTH PLAN FOR INITIATING CONVERSATION

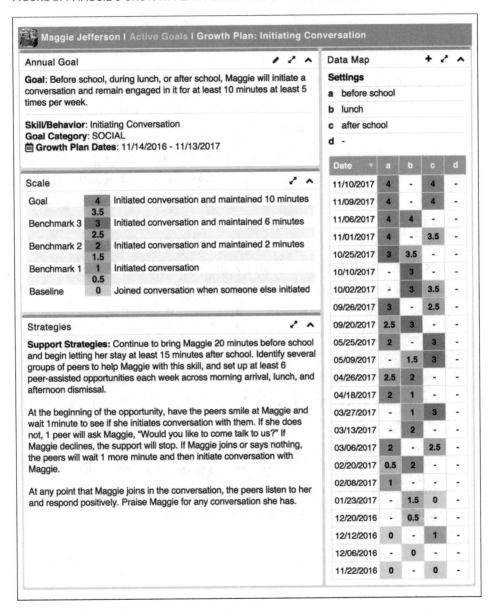

Maggie Jefferson I Active Goals I Growth Plan: Initiating Conversation

Annual Goal

Goal: Before school, during lunch, or after school, Maggie will initiate a conversation and remain engaged in it for at least 10 minutes at least 5 times per week.

Skill/Behavior: Initiating Conversation
Goal Category: SOCIAL
🗓 **Growth Plan Dates**: 11/14/2016 - 11/13/2017

Scale

Goal	4	Initiated conversation and maintained 10 minutes
	3.5	
Benchmark 3	3	Initiated conversation and maintained 6 minutes
	2.5	
Benchmark 2	2	Initiated conversation and maintained 2 minutes
	1.5	
Benchmark 1	1	Initiated conversation
	0.5	
Baseline	0	Joined conversation when someone else initiated

Strategies

Support Strategies: Continue to bring Maggie 20 minutes before school and begin letting her stay at least 15 minutes after school. Identify several groups of peers to help Maggie with this skill, and set up at least 6 peer-assisted opportunities each week across morning arrival, lunch, and afternoon dismissal.

At the beginning of the opportunity, have the peers smile at Maggie and wait 1minute to see if she initiates conversation with them. If she does not, 1 peer will ask Maggie, "Would you like to come talk to us?" If Maggie declines, the support will stop. If Maggie joins or says nothing, the peers will wait 1 more minute and then initiate conversation with Maggie.

At any point that Maggie joins in the conversation, the peers listen to her and respond positively. Praise Maggie for any conversation she has.

Data Map

Settings
a before school
b lunch
c after school
d -

Date	a	b	c	d
11/10/2017	4	-	4	-
11/09/2017	4	-	4	-
11/06/2017	4	4	-	-
11/01/2017	4	-	3.5	-
10/25/2017	3	3.5	-	-
10/10/2017	-	3	-	-
10/02/2017	-	3	3.5	-
09/26/2017	3	-	2.5	-
09/20/2017	2.5	3	-	-
05/25/2017	2	-	3	-
05/09/2017	-	1.5	3	-
04/26/2017	2.5	2	-	-
04/18/2017	2	1	-	-
03/27/2017	-	1	3	-
03/13/2017	-	2	-	-
03/06/2017	2	-	2.5	-
02/20/2017	0.5	2	-	-
02/08/2017	1	-	-	-
01/23/2017	-	1.5	0	-
12/20/2016	-	0.5	-	-
12/12/2016	0	-	1	-
12/06/2016	-	0	-	-
11/22/2016	0	-	0	-

to the strategies being used at the time. This step ensures that both the current support team as well as future ones can see what worked well and what did not.

Questions for Reflection

Think of a student in your school who has autism. What are some of the ways the planning process for this student compares and contrasts to the planning process for Maggie? Specifically, consider the following:

1. Was the planning process used as highly individualized as the one for Maggie? What are some of the barriers to this kind of individualized process? What are some potential solutions for overcoming these barriers?

2. How do you think general education teachers would respond to having these strategies available for use in their classes for a student with autism? Would they embrace them, or see this kind of support as the responsibility of a special education teacher? If the latter, how might you support a cultural shift in your school away from an "our kids"/"their kids" mindset?

3. In serving students with autism, there is a significant trend toward applied behavioral analysis (ABA) therapy. Is this the case in your school? If so, how might you facilitate understanding of the use of behavior support strategies that are ABA-influenced but designed and implemented by an interdisciplinary team and in a more holistic way? How can they be implemented sensibly in a school that is moving to restorative justice practices as a Tier 1 approach?

APPENDIX C
Growth Planning for Danielle

Danielle is a 3rd grade student who is behind grade level in the areas of decoding and reading fluency. Even though she reads at a much slower pace than her peers, her reading comprehension is strong. Danielle, like most students who need support, does *not* have a diagnosed learning disability and doesn't qualify for special education services or an IEP.

Danielle's school uses a response to instruction and intervention (RTI[2]) model and provides her with supplemental reading instruction. For the past six weeks, she has been receiving 30 minutes of direct instruction three times per week in a small group of other struggling readers. Danielle's reading specialist, Judy, uses a curriculum-based measure for twice-weekly progress monitoring. Although Judy estimates that Danielle is currently reading at a mid–1st grade level, she is making marked progress with small-group intervention.

The Team Meeting

Judy, the reading specialist, set up the meeting with Danielle's mother, Charlene. Trisha, the 3rd grade teacher, kicked off the conversation by noting that even though Danielle reads at a much slower pace than is typical in 3rd grade, she'd made a great deal of progress during the past six weeks of intervention. "Still," Trisha said, "I'd like to see Danielle progress at an even faster rate." At this point, Judy described how she conducted the small-group instruction. "Danielle seems to enjoy reading time," she noted. "She is always so well behaved and tries very hard throughout the whole session."

Judy went on to explain that she'd like to increase the frequency of the extra reading sessions from three times per week to five times. "Danielle is doing quite well, but I think she can gain words even faster. And with more intense support, I think she can read faster, too. What do you think about that?" she asked Danielle's mother.

"I think it's great to get her as much help as we can, so that's fine," Charlene replied. She paused, then asked "Do you think this will get Danielle to the same level as the others in the class? You don't think she has a problem that keeps her from being able to read, do you?"

Judy explained, "Many students have a hard time learning to read—and with other skills. Some of these students have neurologically based learning differences, but most do not. Most students who have difficulty learning to read respond well to intervention and don't have any future trouble with reading or with other skills in school."

Charlene looked relieved and said, "Even though Danielle can't read very much, she likes looking at books. She loves it when her grandma reads to her." Judy added, "And she loves to read fantasy stories that feature girls, I've noticed."

Target Area: Reading Fluency

Judy, the reading specialist, shared that Danielle was currently reading at a pace of around 30 words per minute. She talked a little about Danielle's reading fluency, and Trisha gave the team information on a Common Core State Standard for fluency at the 3rd grade level (RF.3.4):

Read with sufficient accuracy and fluency to support comprehension.
a. Read grade-level text with purpose and understanding.
b. Read grade-level prose and poetry orally with accuracy, appropriate rate, and expression on successive readings.
c. Use context to confirm or self-correct word recognition and understanding, rereading as necessary. (NGA & CCSSO, 2010a, p. 17)

Target Area: Sight Words

Judy talked more about what she'd learned in her small-group reading work with Danielle: "So, we've identified that what Danielle seems to struggle with the most is reading pace, and I have a pretty good idea of why that is. I've noticed that she takes a long time to sound out and read individual words, and she's taking time to do this with words that should be in her sight word vocabulary." The team agreed that if Danielle knew all the 3rd grade sight words, her reading pace would greatly improve.

Target Area: Intonation When Reading Aloud

Trisha added, "When Danielle reads, she also doesn't pause for commas or ending punctuation. Even though she has good reading comprehension right now, I imagine that blurring across punctuation like this could eventually disrupt her understanding of the text. When she reads aloud, it is difficult for her to communicate with meaning because she's overlooking the punctuation." Charlene said she'd noticed the same thing, describing Danielle's reading as "robotic."

Priorities

With three critical skills identified, it was time to discuss annual goals.

Charlene turned to her daughter's teachers and asked, "What kind of improvement do you think she will have with extra reading every day?" Judy replied that with daily reading intervention, Danielle should be able to read at a pace of 80 words per minute this time next year. "I'm betting we can have her on grade level in 5th grade," Judy said. "Part of what we need to work on directly is Danielle's sight words. We can do that at school, but you can work on that with her some at home, too." With these two areas of need addressed, the team agreed that they would also set a goal targeting Danielle's need to attend to punctuation when reading.

Figure C.1 shows the critical skills and annual goals set for Danielle.

FIGURE C.1 CRITICAL SKILLS AND ANNUAL GOALS FOR DANIELLE

Critical Skills	Annual Goals
Increasing reading fluency	During language arts, social studies, and science, Danielle will consistently read grade-level text with vocabulary she knows at a rate of 80 words per minute.
Mastering 3rd grade sight words	During language arts and learning support class, Danielle will correctly ready all 41 sight words for 3rd grade within 2 seconds of being presented the word, 10 times in a row.
Pausing for commas and periods when reading aloud	During reading in small and large groups and in learning support class, Danielle will read 3 paragraphs of text, pausing for commas and ending punctuation, every time she reads aloud.

Strategies

While discussing Danielle's reading fluency, Judy described the direct instruction strategy she had been using in small-group reading instruction. She showed everyone an example from the materials she was using and how letter shapes and names and phonics rules are taught. "When a student is reading aloud, the teacher stops the student after any error, gives the correction, and has the student go back to the *beginning* of the sentence to resume reading," Judy explained. The team discussed how this strategy would work for all three of the goals they had prioritized for Danielle.

Danielle's Growth Plans

Danielle's growth plans are shown in Figures C.2, C.3, and C.4.

FIGURE C.2 DANIELLE'S GROWTH PLAN FOR READING FLUENCY

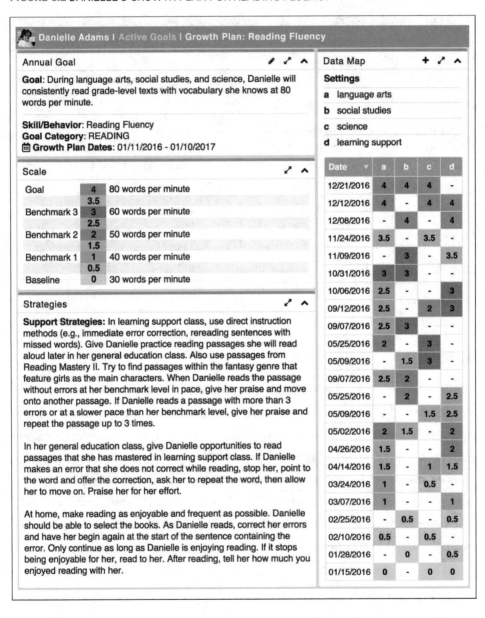

Danielle Adams | Active Goals | Growth Plan: Reading Fluency

Annual Goal

Goal: During language arts, social studies, and science, Danielle will consistently read grade-level texts with vocabulary she knows at 80 words per minute.

Skill/Behavior: Reading Fluency
Goal Category: READING
Growth Plan Dates: 01/11/2016 - 01/10/2017

Scale

Scale	Value	Description
Goal	4	80 words per minute
	3.5	
Benchmark 3	3	60 words per minute
	2.5	
Benchmark 2	2	50 words per minute
	1.5	
Benchmark 1	1	40 words per minute
	0.5	
Baseline	0	30 words per minute

Strategies

Support Strategies: In learning support class, use direct instruction methods (e.g., immediate error correction, rereading sentences with missed words). Give Danielle practice reading passages she will read aloud later in her general education class. Also use passages from Reading Mastery II. Try to find passages within the fantasy genre that feature girls as the main characters. When Danielle reads the passage without errors at her benchmark level in pace, give her praise and move onto another passage. If Danielle reads a passage with more than 3 errors or at a slower pace than her benchmark level, give her praise and repeat the passage up to 3 times.

In her general education class, give Danielle opportunities to read passages that she has mastered in learning support class. If Danielle makes an error that she does not correct while reading, stop her, point to the word and offer the correction, ask her to repeat the word, then allow her to move on. Praise her for her effort.

At home, make reading as enjoyable and frequent as possible. Danielle should be able to select the books. As Danielle reads, correct her errors and have her begin again at the start of the sentence containing the error. Only continue as long as Danielle is enjoying reading. If it stops being enjoyable for her, read to her. After reading, tell her how much you enjoyed reading with her.

Data Map

Settings
a language arts
b social studies
c science
d learning support

Date	a	b	c	d
12/21/2016	4	4	4	-
12/12/2016	4	-	4	4
12/08/2016	-	4	-	4
11/24/2016	3.5	-	3.5	-
11/09/2016	-	3	-	3.5
10/31/2016	3	3	-	-
10/06/2016	2.5	-	-	3
09/12/2016	2.5	-	2	3
09/07/2016	2.5	3	-	-
05/25/2016	2	-	3	-
05/09/2016	-	1.5	3	-
09/07/2016	2.5	2	-	-
05/25/2016	-	2	-	2.5
05/09/2016	-	-	1.5	2.5
05/02/2016	2	1.5	-	2
04/26/2016	1.5	-	-	2
04/14/2016	1.5	-	1	1.5
03/24/2016	1	-	0.5	-
03/07/2016	1	-	-	1
02/25/2016	-	0.5	-	0.5
02/10/2016	0.5	-	0.5	-
01/28/2016	-	0	-	0.5
01/15/2016	0	-	0	0

FIGURE C.3 DANIELLE'S GROWTH PLAN FOR SIGHT WORDS

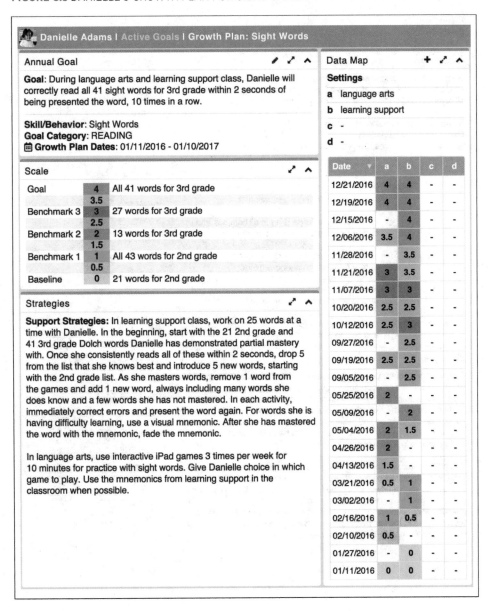

Danielle Adams | Active Goals | **Growth Plan: Sight Words**

Annual Goal

Goal: During language arts and learning support class, Danielle will correctly read all 41 sight words for 3rd grade within 2 seconds of being presented the word, 10 times in a row.

Skill/Behavior: Sight Words
Goal Category: READING
📅 **Growth Plan Dates**: 01/11/2016 - 01/10/2017

Scale

Goal	**4**	All 41 words for 3rd grade
	3.5	
Benchmark 3	**3**	27 words for 3rd grade
	2.5	
Benchmark 2	**2**	13 words for 3rd grade
	1.5	
Benchmark 1	**1**	All 43 words for 2nd grade
	0.5	
Baseline	**0**	21 words for 2nd grade

Strategies

Support Strategies: In learning support class, work on 25 words at a time with Danielle. In the beginning, start with the 21 2nd grade and 41 3rd grade Dolch words Danielle has demonstrated partial mastery with. Once she consistently reads all of these within 2 seconds, drop 5 from the list that she knows best and introduce 5 new words, starting with the 2nd grade list. As she masters words, remove 1 word from the games and add 1 new word, always including many words she does know and a few words she has not mastered. In each activity, immediately correct errors and present the word again. For words she is having difficulty learning, use a visual mnemonic. After she has mastered the word with the mnemonic, fade the mnemonic.

In language arts, use interactive iPad games 3 times per week for 10 minutes for practice with sight words. Give Danielle choice in which game to play. Use the mnemonics from learning support in the classroom when possible.

Data Map

Settings
a language arts
b learning support
c -
d -

Date ▼	a	b	c	d
12/21/2016	4	4	-	-
12/19/2016	4	4	-	-
12/15/2016	-	4	-	-
12/06/2016	3.5	4	-	-
11/28/2016	-	3.5	-	-
11/21/2016	3	3.5	-	-
11/07/2016	3	3	-	-
10/20/2016	2.5	2.5	-	-
10/12/2016	2.5	3	-	-
09/27/2016	-	2.5	-	-
09/19/2016	2.5	2.5	-	-
09/05/2016	-	2.5	-	-
05/25/2016	2	-	-	-
05/09/2016	-	2	-	-
05/04/2016	2	1.5	-	-
04/26/2016	2	-	-	-
04/13/2016	1.5	-	-	-
03/21/2016	0.5	1	-	-
03/02/2016	-	1	-	-
02/16/2016	1	0.5	-	-
02/10/2016	0.5	-	-	-
01/27/2016	-	0	-	-
01/11/2016	0	0	-	-

FIGURE C.4 DANIELLE'S GROWTH PLAN FOR READING INTONATION

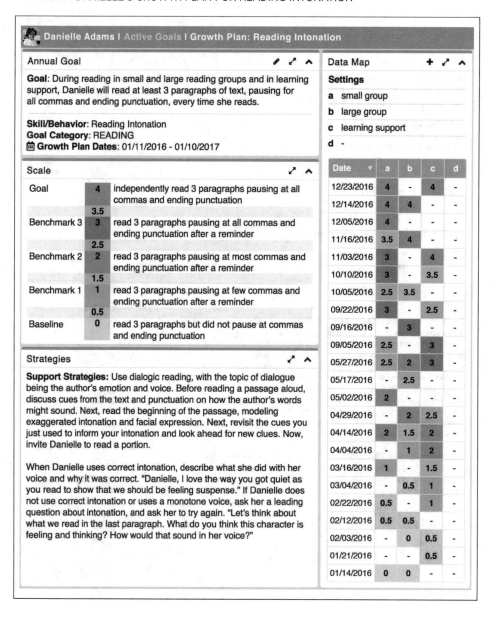

Danielle Adams I Active Goals I Growth Plan: Reading Intonation

Annual Goal

Goal: During reading in small and large reading groups and in learning support, Danielle will read at least 3 paragraphs of text, pausing for all commas and ending punctuation, every time she reads.

Skill/Behavior: Reading Intonation
Goal Category: READING
Growth Plan Dates: 01/11/2016 - 01/10/2017

Scale

Goal	4	independently read 3 paragraphs pausing at all commas and ending punctuation
	3.5	
Benchmark 3	3	read 3 paragraphs pausing at all commas and ending punctuation after a reminder
	2.5	
Benchmark 2	2	read 3 paragraphs pausing at most commas and ending punctuation after a reminder
	1.5	
Benchmark 1	1	read 3 paragraphs pausing at few commas and ending punctuation after a reminder
	0.5	
Baseline	0	read 3 paragraphs but did not pause at commas and ending punctuation

Strategies

Support Strategies: Use dialogic reading, with the topic of dialogue being the author's emotion and voice. Before reading a passage aloud, discuss cues from the text and punctuation on how the author's words might sound. Next, read the beginning of the passage, modeling exaggerated intonation and facial expression. Next, revisit the cues you just used to inform your intonation and look ahead for new clues. Now, invite Danielle to read a portion.

When Danielle uses correct intonation, describe what she did with her voice and why it was correct. "Danielle, I love the way you got quiet as you read to show that we should be feeling suspense." If Danielle does not use correct intonation or uses a monotone voice, ask her a leading question about intonation, and ask her to try again. "Let's think about what we read in the last paragraph. What do you think this character is feeling and thinking? How would that sound in her voice?"

Data Map

Settings
a small group
b large group
c learning support
d -

Date	a	b	c	d
12/23/2016	4	-	4	-
12/14/2016	4	4	-	-
12/05/2016	4	-	-	-
11/16/2016	3.5	4	-	-
11/03/2016	3	-	4	-
10/10/2016	3	-	3.5	-
10/05/2016	2.5	3.5	-	-
09/22/2016	3	-	2.5	-
09/16/2016	-	3	-	-
09/05/2016	2.5	-	3	-
05/27/2016	2.5	2	3	-
05/17/2016	-	2.5	-	-
05/02/2016	2	-	-	-
04/29/2016	-	2	2.5	-
04/14/2016	2	1.5	2	-
04/04/2016	-	1	2	-
03/16/2016	1	-	1.5	-
03/04/2016	-	0.5	1	-
02/22/2016	0.5	-	1	-
02/12/2016	0.5	0.5	-	-
02/03/2016	-	0	0.5	-
01/21/2016	-	-	0.5	-
01/14/2016	0	0	-	-

Team Reflection and Revision

As Danielle's team reflected on her progress in reading fluency, they noticed that she had progressed more quickly in learning support class and language arts than in social studies and science. They also noticed that her growth in intonation (pausing for commas and ending punctuation) was similarly higher in the learning support setting than in the small and large groups within the general 3rd grade classroom.

The team thought through what could be contributing to the differences by discussing how each team member was implementing the strategies. Trisha and Judy each described how they were using the strategies with Danielle and confirmed that the strategies were being implemented with fidelity in the classroom. After a closer examination of these patterns across both the fluency and intonation goals, it became apparent that Danielle was doing well acquiring these language arts skills within the learning support class, but there was a lag in her acquisition of the skills within that setting and in her ability to generalize the skills to other settings. Ultimately, the team decided the plan was working, but they would continue to monitor this pattern to support Danielle's continued growth in the group settings and in social studies and science.

Questions for Reflection

Think of a student in your school who is below grade level on a skill but does not have an IEP. What are some of the ways the planning process for this student compares and contrasts to the planning process for Danielle? Specifically, consider the following:

1. Danielle's teachers came together to plan for her growth much in the same way they would for an IEP, albeit without the formal IEP document. Is there a process for this kind of support in your school? If not, how are teachers measuring the progress that students who are below grade

level but do not have an IEP are making toward the acquisition of critical skills? What kind of interventions are in place to support these students?

2. If students are progressing well in some settings and not in others, one of the contributing factors can be poor or inconsistent implementation of strategies. This can be a complex teaming issue! How could you help a fellow teacher implement intervention strategies with greater fidelity while maintaining a healthy relationship with that person?

3. Danielle's mom, Charlene, was very concerned about seeing Danielle meet grade-level expectations in reading. She wanted to know if it was possible for Danielle to be on grade level soon. How can the process of growth planning help us have conversations with families of students who need support but don't have a diagnosis? This can be difficult when we suspect a disability is possible. How do we support families through this process?

REFERENCES
& RESOURCES

Achieve. (2013). *Next generation science standards.* Washington, DC: Author.

Adams, G., & Carnine, D. (2003). Direct instruction. In. H. L. Swanson, K. R. Harris, & S. Graham (Eds.), *Handbook of learning disabilities* (pp. 403–416). New York: Guilford Press.

Alberto, A. A., & Troutman, A. C. (2003). *Applied behavior analysis for teachers* (6th ed.). Upper Saddle River, NJ: Merrill–Prentice Hall.

Bailey, D. B., Raspa, M., & Fox, L. C. (2012). What is the future of family outcomes and family-centered services? *Topics in Early Childhood Special Education, 31*(4), 216–223.

Bondy, A. S., & Frost, L. A. (1994). The Picture Exchange Communication System. *Focus on Autism and Other Developmental Disabilities, 9*(3), 1–19. doi: 10.1177/108835769400900301

Bronfenbrenner, U. (1977). Toward an experimental ecology of human development. *American Psychologist, 32*(7), 513–531. doi:10.1037/0003-066X.32.7.513

Cooper, J. O., Heron, T. E., & Heward, W. L. (2007). *Applied behavior analysis* (2nd ed.). Upper Saddle River, NJ: Pearson/Merrill–Prentice Hall.

Cordova, D. I., & Lepper, M. R. (1996). Intrinsic motivation and the process of learning: Beneficial effects of contextualization, personalization, and choice. *Journal of Educational Psychology, 88*(4), 715–730.

Cox, J. A., & Boren, L. M. (1965). A study of backward chaining. *Journal of Educational Psychology, 56*(5), 270–274.

Cytrynbaum, S., Ginath, Y., Birdwell, J., & Brandt, L. (1979). Goal attainment scaling: A critical review. *Evaluation Quarterly, 3*(1), 5–40.

Data Accountability Center. (2010). *Part B child count, 2008.* Retrieved from www.ideadata .org/PartBChildCount.asp

Ellis, E. S. (1994). Integrating writing strategy instruction with content-area instruction: Part II—Writing processes. *Intervention in School and Clinic, 29*(4), 219–228. doi: 10.1177/105345129402900406

Endrew F. v. Douglas County School District, 580 U. S. 2017. Retrieved from https://supreme .justia.com/cases/federal/us/580/15-827/opinion3.html

Engelmann, S., & Bruner, E. C. (1969). *Distar reading I: An instructional system.* Chicago: Science Research Associates.

Etscheidt, S. K. (2006). Progress monitoring: Legal issues and recommendations for IEP teams. *Teaching Exceptional Children, 38*(3), 56–60.

Fletcher, J. M. (2006). The need for response to instruction models of learning disabilities. *Perspectives on Language and Literacy, 32,* 12–15.

Freedman (2005). *Grades, report cards, etc. . . . And the law.* Boston: School Law Pro.

Fuchs, D., Fuchs, L. S., Al Otaiba, S., Thompson, A., Yen, L., McMaster, K. N., Svenson, E., & Yang, N. J. (2001). K-PALS: Helping kindergartners with reading readiness: Teachers and researchers in partnerships. *Teaching Exceptional Children, 33*(4), 76–80.

Fuchs, D., Fuchs, L. S., & Burish, P. (2000). Peer-assisted learning strategies: An evidence-based practice to promote reading achievement. *Learning Disabilities Research and Practice, 15,* 85–91.

Fuchs, D., Fuchs, L. S., Mathes, P. G., & Simmons, D. C. (1997). Peer-assisted learning strategies: Making classrooms more responsive to diversity. *American Educational Research Journal, 34*(1), 174.

Fuchs, D., Fuchs, L. S., & Vaughn, S. (2014). What is intensive instruction and why is it important? *Teaching Exceptional Children, 46*(4), 13–18.

Fuchs, L. S., Fuchs, D., & Kazdan, S. (1999). Effects of peer-assisted learning strategies on high school students with serious reading problems. *Remedial and Special Education, 20,* 309–318.

Giangreco, M. F., Cloninger, C. J., & Iverson, V. S. (1993). *Choosing options and accommodations for children: A guide to planning inclusive education.* Baltimore: Brooks.

Gleason, K. A., Kwok, O. M., & Hughes, J. N. (2007). The short-term effect of grade retention on peer relations and academic performance of at-risk first graders. *Elementary School Journal, 107*(4), 327–340.

Gray, C. (1993). Social stories: Improving responses of students with autism with accurate social information. *Focus on Autistic Behavior, 8,* 1–10.

Haring, N., Liberty, K., & White, O. (1978). *Third annual report: Field initiated research studies of phases of learning and facilitating instructional events for the severely/ profoundly handicapped.* (U.S. Department of Education, Contract No. G007500593.) Seattle: University of Washington.

Hart, S. L., & Banda, D. R. (2010). Picture exchange communication system with individuals with developmental disabilities: A meta-analysis of single subject studies. *Remedial and Special Education, 31*(6), 476–488. doi:10.1177/0741932509338354

Hattie, J. (2012). *Visible learning for teachers: Maximizing impact on learning.* New York: Routledge.

Hughes, J. N., Kwok, O. M., & Im, M. H. (2013). Effect of retention in first grade on parents' educational expectations and children's academic outcomes. *American Educational Research Journal, 50*(6), 349–365.

Individuals with Disabilities Education Improvement Act, 20 U.S.C § 1400 to 1482 (2004).

Iwata, B. A., Pace, G. M., Cowdery, G. E., Miltenberger, R. G. (1994). What makes extinction work: An analysis of procedural form & function. *Journal of Applied Behavior Analysis, 27*(1), 131–144.

Jung, L. A. (2007a). Writing individualized family service plan strategies that fit into the ROUTINE. *Young Exceptional Children, 10*(3), 2–9.

Jung, L. A. (2007b). Writing SMART objectives and strategies that fit the ROUTINE. *Teaching Exceptional Children, 39*(4), 54–58.

Jung, L. A. (2010). Can embedding prompts in the IFSP form improve the quality of IFSPs developed? *Journal of Early Intervention, 32*(3), 200–213.

Jung, L. A. (2017a, April 27). *How can goal attainment scaling help schools respond to Endrew v. Douglas County?* ASCD Student Growth Center. Retrieved from https://www.studentgrowth.org/2017/04/25/goal-attainment-scaling-answer-endrew-v-douglas-county

Jung, L. A. (2017b, June). How to keep mutiny from sinking your change effort. *Educational Leadership, 74*(online), 28–32.

Jung, L. A. (2017c, April). In providing supports for students, language matters. *Educational Leadership, 74*(7), 42–45.

Jung, L. A. (2017d, March 11). Retention is not an intervention. ASCD Student Growth Center. Retrieved from https://www.studentgrowth.org/2017/03/11/retention-is-not-an-intervention/

Jung, L. A. (2018, February). Scales of progress. *Educational Leadership, 75*(6), 22–27.

Jung, L. A., Baird, S. M., Gomez, C., & Galyon-Keramidas, C. (2008). Family-centered intervention: Bridging the gap between IEPs and implementation. *Teaching Exceptional Children, 41*(1), 26–33.

Mackey, A., & Philp, J. (1998). Conversational interaction and second language development: Recasts, responses, and red herrings? *Modern Language Journal, 82*(3), 338–356.

McClannahan, L. E., & Krantz, P. J. (2010). *Activity schedules for children with autism: Teaching independent behavior* (2nd ed.). Bethesda, MD: Woodbine House.

Meyen, E. L., Vergason, G. A., & Whelan, R. J. (1996). *Strategies for teaching exceptional children in inclusive settings.* Denver: Love.

Morgan, P. L., & Meier, C. R. (2008). Dialogic reading's potential to improve children's emergent literacy skills and behavior. *Preventing School Failure, 52*(4), 11–16.

Moss, C. M., & Brookhart, S. M. (2009). *Advancing formative assessment in every classroom: A guide for instructional leaders.* Alexandria, VA: ASCD.

National Center for Education Statistics. (2013). Elementary and secondary education. In *Digest of education statistics, 2012* (NCES 2014–015, pp. 63–306). Retrieved from http://nces.ed.gov/pubs2014/2014015.pdf

National Council for the Social Studies (NCSS). (2013). *The College, Career, and Civic Life (C3) framework for social studies state standards: Guidance for enhancing the rigor of K–12 civics, economics, geography, and history.* Silver Spring, MD: Author.

National Governors Association (NGA) Center for Best Practices & Council of Chief State School Officers (CCSSO). (2010a). *Common Core State Standards for English language arts & literacy in history/social studies, science, and technical subjects.* Washington, DC: Authors. Retrieved from www.corestandards.org/assets/CCSSI_ELA%20Standards .pdf.

National Governors Association (NGA) Center for Best Practices & Council of Chief State School Officers (CCSSO). (2010b). *Read the standards.* Washington, DC: Authors. Retrieved from http://www.corestandards.org/read-the-standards/

Neitzel, J. (2009). *Overview of time delay.* Chapel Hill, NC: National Professional Development Center on Autism Spectrum Disorders, Frank Porter Graham Child Development Institute, The University of North Carolina at Chapel Hill.

Ruble, L. A., McGrew, J., Dalrymple, N., & Jung, L. A. (2010). Examining the quality of IEPs for young children with autism. *Journal of Autism, 40*(12), 1459–1470.

Ruble, L. A., McGrew, J., Toland, M., Dalrymple, N., & Jung, L. A. (2013). A randomized controlled trial of COMPASS web-based and face-to-face teacher coaching in autism. *Journal of Consulting and Clinical Psychology, 81*(3), 566–572.

Rupley, W. H., Blair, T. R., & Nichols, W. D. (2009). Effective reading instruction for struggling readers: The role of direct/explicit teaching. *Reading and Writing Quarterly, 25*(2–3), 125–138.

Sanches-Ferreira, M., Lopes-dos-Santos, P., Alves, S., Santos, M., & Silveira-Maia, M. (2013). How individualised are the individualised education programmes (IEPs): An analysis of the contents and quality of the IEP goals. *European Journal of Special Needs Education, 28*(4), 507–520.

Schmid, C. F. (1954). *Handbook of graphic presentation.* New York: Ronald Press.

Shabani, D. B., Wilder, D. A., & Flood, W. A. (2001). Reducing stereotypic behavior through discrimination training, differential reinforcement of other behavior, and self-monitoring. *Behavioral Interventions, 16*(4), 279–286.

Snow, K. (2014). *Disability is natural: Revolutionary common sense about people with disabilities* [Video]. Available from http://disabilityisnatural.com/

Spörer, N., Brunstein, J. C., & Kieschke, U. (2009). Improving students' reading comprehension skills: Effects of strategy instruction and reciprocal teaching. *Learning and Instruction, 19*(3), 272–286. doi:10.1016/j.learninstruc.2008.05.003

Watson, T. S., & Steege, M. W. (2003). *Conducting school-based functional behavioral assessments: A practitioner's guide.* New York: Guilford Press.

Weinstein, C. E., & Mayer, R. E. (1986). The teaching of learning strategies. In M. C. Wittrock (Ed.), *Handbook of research on teaching* (3rd ed.) (pp. 315–327). New York: Macmillan.

Whitehurst, G. J., Epstein, J. N., Angel, A. L., Payne, A. C., & Al, E. (1994). Outcomes of an emergent literacy intervention in Head Start. *Journal of Educational Psychology, 86*(4), 542–555. doi: 10.1037/0022-0663.86.4.542

Wolgemuth, J. R., Cobb, R. B., & Alwell, M. (2008). The effects of mnemonic interventions on academic outcomes for youth with disabilities: A systematic review. *Learning Disabilities Research, 23*(1), 1–10.

INDEX

Note: Page references followed by an italicized *f* indicates information contained in figures.

ABOUT THE AUTHOR

 **Lee Ann Jung, PhD,** is Chief Academic Officer and Co-Founder of ASCD Student Growth Center, which produces GoalWorks® progress monitoring software. She provides support internationally to schools in the areas of inclusion, standards-based grading, and intervention planning and progress monitoring. She has worked in the field of special education since 1994 and has served in the roles of teacher, administrator, consultant, and professor and director of International School Partnerships at the University of Kentucky.

Dr. Jung is chair of the Classroom Assessment Special Interest Group for the American Educational Research Association. She has authored or coauthored 5 books and more than 40 journal articles and book chapters, and has been awarded more than $4 million in federal funding to support personnel preparation and research. She has served as associate editor for *Young Exceptional Children* (YEC), guest editor and editorial board member of *Topics in Early Childhood Special Education*, and editorial board member for *Journal of Early Intervention*. She can be reached at jung@studentgrowth.org.

Related Resources

At the time of publication, the following resources were available (ASCD stock numbers in parentheses):

PD Online® Courses
Inclusion: The Basics, 2nd Edition (#PD11OC121M)
Inclusion: Implementing Strategies, 2nd Edition (#PD11OC122M)

Print Products
A Teacher's Guide to Special Education by David Bateman and Jenifer L. Cline (#116019)
Building on the Strengths of Students with Special Needs: How to Move Beyond Disability Labels in the Classroom by Toby Karten (#117023)
Causes & Cures in the Classroom: Getting to the Root of Academic and Behavior Problems by Margaret Searle (#113019)
Enhancing RTI: How to Ensure Success with Effective Classroom Instruction and Intervention by Douglas Fisher and Nancy Frey (#111037)
Hanging In: Strategies for Teaching the Students Who Challenge Us Most by Jeffrey Benson (#114013)
Inclusion Dos, Don'ts, and Do Betters (Quick Reference Guide) by Toby J. Karten (#QRG116082)
Leading an Inclusive School: Access and Success for ALL Students by Richard A. Villa and Jacqueline S. Thousand (#116022)
Success with IEPs: Solving Five Common Implementation Challenges in the Classroom (ASCD Arias) by Vicki Caruana (#SF117047)
Teaching in Tandem: Effective Co-Teaching in the Inclusive Classroom by Joan Blednik and Gloria Lodata Wilson (#110029)

For up-to-date information about ASCD resources, go to www.ascd.org. You can search the complete archives of Educational Leadership at www.ascd.org/el.

ASCD myTeachSource®
Download resources from a professional learning platform with hundreds of research-based best practices and tools for your classroom at http://myteachsource.ascd.org/

For more information, send an e-mail to member@ascd.org; call 1-800-933-2723 or 703-578-9600; send a fax to 703-575-5400; or write to Information Services, ASCD, 1703 N. Beauregard St., Alexandria, VA 22311-1714 USA.